Bucking the Deficit

Dilemmas in American Politics

Series Editor   **L. Sandy Maisel,** *Colby College*

Dilemmas in American Politics offers teachers and students a series of quality books on timely topics and key institutions in American government. Each text will examine a "real world" dilemma and will be structured to cover the historical, theoretical, policy relevant, and future dimensions of its subject.

BOOKS IN THIS SERIES

FORTHCOMING TITLES

Bucking the Deficit

Economic Policymaking in America

G. Calvin Mackenzie &
Saranna Thornton
Colby College

 WestviewPress
A Division of HarperCollins*Publishers*

Dilemmas in American Politics

Copyright © 1996 by Westview Press, Inc., A Division of HarperCollins Publishers, Inc.

Published in 1996 in the United States of America by Westview Press, Inc., 5500 Central Avenue, Boulder, Colorado 80301-2877, and in the United Kingdom by Westview Press, 12 Hid's Copse Road, Cumnor Hill, Oxford OX2 9JJ

Library of Congress Cataloging-in-Publication Data
Mackenzie, G. Calvin.
    Bucking the deficit : economic policymaking in America / G. Calvin
Mackenzie & Saranna Thornton.
       p.   cm. — (Dilemmas in American politics)
    Includes bibliographical references and index.
    ISBN 0-8133-2060-7 (hardcover). — ISBN 0-8133-2061-5 (pbk.).
    1. United States—economic policy.   2. Budget deficits—United
States—History—20th century.   3. Finance, Public—United States—
History—20th century.   I. Thornton, Saranna.   II. Title.
III. Series.
HC106.M23   1996
338.973—dc20   95-41949
                                                                                                              CIP

The paper used in this publication meets the requirements of the American National Standard for Permanence of Paper for Printed Library Materials Z39.48-1984.

10   9   8   7   6   5   4   3   2   1

Contents

4 Dilemmas of Contemporary Economic Policy

Illustrations

Tables

Figures

Boxes

Cartoons

Preface

EVERYWHERE THESE DAYS the talk is of money. Candidates promise more jobs, lower taxes, less government spending, and a smaller federal deficit. Political leaders wrangle endlessly over budgets. Even issues such as crime, health care, welfare reform, and foreign policy quickly evolve into money matters: How much should we spend, how much can we afford?

The simple reality is that no one can begin to understand contemporary politics without first learning about the relationship between government and the American economy. Although America's economy remains one of the freest in the world, the twentieth century has changed it significantly. The federal government now spends more than 20 percent of the money that circulates through the economy each year. The government regulates nearly every industry and many business practices. American banks are privately owned, but the government dictates many of their practices. American citizens drive on roads built with government funds, talk on telephones regulated by government agencies, send their mail through the government's post office, and pay sizable chunks of their earnings in government taxes. The modern economy and the modern polity grow ever more entangled.

In this book, we offer students of American politics an introduction to the American political economy. This is a broad and complex subject, and we have not covered every aspect of it here. But the chapters that follow will help to acquaint readers with the principal concepts, the most prominent theories, the primary processes, and the language of American economic policy.

Chapter 1 focuses on the basics: the character of the American free market economy, how markets form and wealth is accumulated, the role of money, and the impact of government economic decisions. In the second half of the chapter we explore the economic theories that have shaped policymaking in the twentieth century: classical liberalism, Keynesianism, monetarism, and supply-side analysis.

Chapter 2 offers an overview of economic policy development during the past century, a century of gradual but sweeping economic changes. Chapter 2 focuses on the critical turning points: the Populist and Progressive movements around the turn of the century, the New Deal and the world wars, and the extraordinary postwar economic boom.

In Chapter 3 we concentrate on the principal avenues of economic policymaking. We explore fiscal policy and the budget; monetary policy and the Federal Reserve System; microeconomic policy, including regulation, subsidies, credit, and industrial policy; and international trade.

Chapter 4 is an examination of some of the most important dilemmas and constraints faced by contemporary economic policymakers. How do they cope with theoretical and analytical uncertainty? How can the efforts of so many economic actors be effectively coordinated? How do economic policymakers deal with input overload in an increasingly complex political system? Can policymakers tame the entitlement, pork-barrel, and deficit monsters that seem to devour all new policy initiatives? And finally, what price do we pay for an economic-policy process that seems resistant to bold change?

Chapter 5 concludes this book with an exploration of three future scenarios for American economic policy. What will happen if we make no significant changes in the way economic policy is constructed, if we stick with politics as usual? Or what might happen if we undertake broad reforms of the sort many people are now recommending? Or suppose we continue simply to muddle through, to do what is minimally necessary to stave off the next crisis?

American economic policymaking is at an important historical turning point. But it is not at all clear that the American political system is capable of turning. Hence the topics raised in this book are the central issues of contemporary political combat and concern. We hope this book helps readers in their attempts to understand these issues and encourages them to more fully and wisely participate in the critical debates that swirl around them.

G. Calvin Mackenzie
Saranna Thornton

Acknowledgments

WE INCURRED MANY debts in writing this book, and we are pleased to acknowledge them here.

At Colby, we were blessed by the diligent and creative research assistance we received from Colin Harrington, Sandra Hughes, Chrisanne Loll, Adam Muller, and Chris Selicious.

Our colleagues in the Colby Economics and Government Departments were, as always, a constant source of stimulation, ideas, valuable criticism, and fun. Although many of their contributions were indirect, their wisdom informs every page of this book.

We are especially grateful to our colleague, L. Sandy Maisel, the William R. Kenan Jr. Professor of Government at Colby, who encouraged us to write this book and offered valuable suggestions and critiques along the way.

Our friends at Westview Press were supportive, creative, and extraordinarily efficient throughout this project. We especially acknowledge those fine professionals with whom we dealt directly: Jennifer Knerr, Eric Wright, Brenda Hadenfeldt, and Shena Redmond.

Several anonymous readers did their job with real skill. Their criticisms and suggestions directed us and our readers around a number of potential pitfalls. Diane Hess was an excellent copy editor whose keen eye sharpened this manuscript in many ways.

Finally, we want to acknowledge the most important contributors to this work: the Colby students whose questions and comments over many years have helped us to understand what it is about the American economy that most needs explaining. In many ways the words that appear here represent refinements of our efforts to respond intelligently to the vexing issues that Colby students have raised in our classes. Some of them will read this book and realize that our conversations continue.

To all of these people, we express our deep thanks.

G.C.M.
S.T.

1

....

The American Economy: Concepts and Theories

If all economists were laid end to end,
they would not reach a conclusion.

—George Bernard Shaw

On JANUARY 7, 1993, President-elect Bill Clinton met with his economic advisers and was told that an economic program of spending cuts and tax hikes that would *credibly* shrink the budget deficit would also influence U.S. financial markets to reduce long-term interest rates. Lower long-term interest rates, in turn, would stimulate the economy and reduce the unemployment rate. The advisers also instructed Clinton that the reverse was true. A program composed only of political gimmicks would spook the financial markets, generating increases in long-term interest rates that could abort the anemic economic recovery then under way. Clinton raged: "You mean to tell me that the success of the program and my reelection hinges on the Federal Reserve and a bunch of . . . bond traders?" The advisers nodded their heads yes (Woodward, 1994, p. 84).

Clinton accepted their advice, jettisoning some of his campaign promises for increased government spending and a middle-class tax cut. These promises were inconsistent with the new goal of deficit reduction.

President Clinton faced the central dilemma of economic policymaking—in many ways, the central dilemma of late-twentieth-century American politics: how to balance the desire of the American people for more and better public programs with their desire for a progressively less expensive government. Americans like the benefits, but not the costs, of government. Often, in fact, Americans—encouraged by their political leaders—neglect to see the connections between the costs and benefits of government.

In restaurants across America, there are signs that say, "Please pay when served." In doctors' offices, similar signs say, "Payment is expected when service is rendered." No such signs hang in federal government offices. The provision of services and payment for those services are disconnected. In fact, most of the benefits we receive from government require no direct payment from the beneficiary. They are public goods, and their costs are borne broadly by the whole population, or at least the tax-paying portion of it. None of us makes direct payment to the air traffic controllers who bring our planes in safely, to the inspectors at the Food and Drug Administration who ensure the safety of the products we consume, or to the Coast Guard crews who place the buoys that mark dangerous shoals. We pay for those services diffusely and indirectly through our taxes.

In fact, we often pay for less than we get because we don't like to pay taxes and our elected leaders don't like to impose them on us—not if they want to continue to be our elected leaders. So the government has acquired the habit of spending more public funds than it raises from taxes and other revenues. The gap is filled by borrowing money to cover all obligations. In government, this is called deficit spending.

We've become accustomed to deficit spending in the years since 1970. We've never had a budget surplus or even a balanced budget in that period. In the twenty-five fiscal years starting in 1970, our deficits totaled $3.17 trillion.

By 1992, when President Clinton was elected, the jig was up. The size of the annual deficit, and the growing burden of paying for earlier deficits, had become the dominant factors in all of American policymaking. No program initiative or tax change could be undertaken without first considering its impact on the deficit. For political leaders, the central dilemma was this: How can we do the things government ought to do, the things that citizens want their government to do, in the face of the enormous economic constraints created by a quarter-century of deficit spending? That is the subject of this book, and it is precisely the dilemma Bill Clinton faced in the first month—and in every subsequent month—of his presidency.

Many people realize that the economic programs of the federal government affect the state of the economy. In fact, people often believe—falsely—that the president exerts direct control over the economy through these programs. On the contrary, in the United States there is a complex and dynamic relationship between the economy and the government's economic policy.

To understand this relationship it is necessary to begin with some basic concepts of economic analysis and to explore the economic-policy prescriptions of some of the major economic theories. How does the American economy work? How does it compare with other national economies? How do we measure its vitality and its patterns and pace of change? Those are the questions we seek to answer in this chapter.

Important Economic Terms and Tools

What Is a Free Market Economy?

The economies of the former Soviet Union and other countries in eastern Europe have begun to dismantle their **command economies.** In a command economy, the government determines what is produced and in what quantity, what methods of production are utilized, and what prices are charged. The countries of eastern Europe are abandoning their command economies to adopt **free market economies.** The transformation is painful, involving large social costs—unemployment, price increases, and uncertainty. Why are the peoples of these countries willing to bear such costs? Because free market economies promise benefits that command economies have never been able to secure and sustain.

A **market** is a structured environment in which buyers and sellers exchange goods or services, usually for money. Markets exist to promote an efficient exchange of items of value. For example, the store where you order pizza is a market. Likewise, the vending machine where you buy a soda before class is a market. Markets can be local or international in scope. But in all markets it is the *interactions* of buyers and sellers that determine what is produced, how it is produced, who receives the output of production, and what price they pay.

A free market economy is one in which the government plays no role in exchanges between buyers and sellers. It is characterized by unregulated markets. The U.S. economy hardly fits this description. It is not a pure free market economy. But on the spectrum between a command economy and a free market economy, the United States remains much closer to a free market economy. In fact, political leaders in America argue constantly about how "free" the free market economy should be. In the 1990s, for example, many Republicans in Congress have introduced or supported proposals that would reduce the federal government's role in the economy, that would make the free market even more free from constraints imposed by government.

An efficient allocation of resources (e.g., labor, machinery, natural resources) is one major advantage of a free market economy. Competition normally guides resources into the production of goods and services that society wants most. In recent years, for example, consumer power has dictated that few resources go into the production of records because people now prefer to hear their music on compact disc or audiocassette. As firms compete to stay profitable they will seek to provide the most desired goods and services and to adopt the most efficient means of production. With ample competition, consumers will usually be able to purchase goods and services for the lowest possible prices. Think, for example, about how the past decade's price wars between personal computer manufacturers dramatically lowered the price of PCs.

These benefits lead most economists to argue against government regulation of free markets. All but the most rigid economists will admit, however, that government regulation may be necessary under some circumstances:

Demise of Competition. When competition declines among firms in specific economic sectors, so that fewer firms are selling a product or service, the power of consumers also declines. This results in higher prices and an insufficient supply of the product being produced. For example, a federal judge ruled that domination of the national telephone system by AT&T denied adequate competition and consumer choice. In 1982, AT&T agreed to divest itself of twenty-two smaller companies that came to be known as the Baby Bells. These companies, and others that soon emerged, dramatically altered the options for consumers in telephone services and hardware.

Unequal Distribution of Income. Some people in a free market economy find themselves unable to purchase even the most basic necessities. At the 1995 minimum wage of $4.25, a person working full time would earn, before taxes, $170 a week, or $8,840 per year. Imagine trying to support yourself on that or, worse, trying to support a family! Figure 1.1 illustrates the distribution of in-

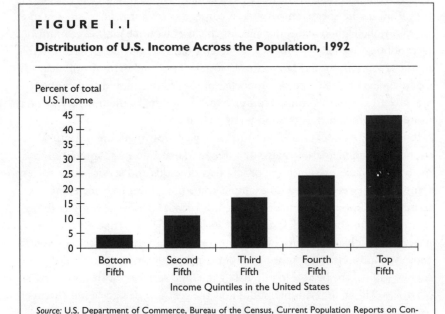

FIGURE 1.1

Distribution of U.S. Income Across the Population, 1992

Percent of total
U.S. Income

Income Quintiles in the United States
(Bottom Fifth, Second Fifth, Third Fifth, Fourth Fifth, Top Fifth)

Source: U.S. Department of Commerce, Bureau of the Census, Current Population Reports on Consumer Income, *Money Income of Households, Families, and Persons in the United States: 1992* (Washington, D.C.: Government Printing Office, 1993), p. B6.

come across the U.S. population. Examining the two extremes, we see that the 20 percent of the population at the top of the scale earns almost 45 percent of all U.S. income. In contrast, the 20 percent of the population at the bottom of the scale earns less than 5 percent of all U.S. income.

Sometimes an unequal distribution of income in society results from discrimination or other imperfections in the free market. In these cases income inequality is usually thought to be unfair and citizens turn to the government for solutions. Additionally, some economic studies suggest that economic growth is retarded by an unequal distribution of income (Chang, 1994). In this case an unequal distribution of income negatively affects everyone in society.

In an attempt to alleviate this problem the government uses a variety of regulatory, spending, and tax programs including job training, college loans, and the earned-income tax credit, which provides supplemental income to individuals who work but still can't earn an adequate living. As illustrated by Figure 1.2, the success of government policies has been mixed. From 1947 through 1973, social welfare programs, greater government enforcement of civil rights, the GI Bill, and other government measures promoted equal growth in inflation-adjusted income across all population groups. During this period of time, income inequality declined.

This trend changed dramatically beginning in the 1970s. From 1973 through 1992 the inflation-adjusted income of the top 20 percent of the U.S. population grew by almost 20 percent. In contrast, income of the bottom 20 percent of the U.S. population declined by more than 10 percent. The distribution of income during this time became more unequal. The disparity was exacerbated by the economic policies of the Reagan administration, which included reductions in government spending on social programs, reductions in personal income tax rates that favored the wealthy, and increases in social insurance taxes (i.e., Social Security) that imposed a greater relative burden on the poor and middle class.

Market Failure: Externalities. For certain goods and services, prices determined in the free market fail to reflect all the costs of production or all the benefits that the product generates. The additional costs or benefits associated with products of this type are borne not by the seller or buyer, but by a third party. Those costs or benefits are external to the transaction, hence the term **externalities.** In situations where substantial benefits accrue not just to the buyer but to a third party, the goods or services in question will be underproduced. For example, consider public schools, which provide direct as well as external benefits. An individual directly benefits from getting an education through the

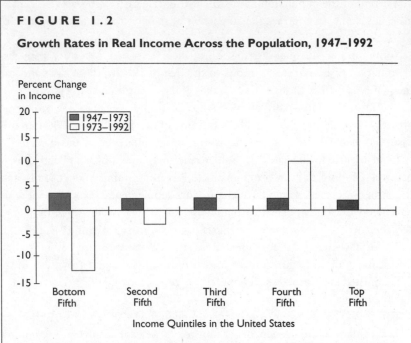

FIGURE 1.2

Growth Rates in Real Income Across the Population, 1947–1992

Percent Change
in Income

Legend: 1947–1973 / 1973–1992

Income Quintiles in the United States

(x-axis categories: Bottom Fifth, Second Fifth, Third Fifth, Fourth Fifth, Top Fifth)

Source: U.S. Department of Commerce, Bureau of the Census, Current Population Reports on Consumer Income, *Money Income of Households, Families, and Persons in the United States: 1992* (Washington, D.C.: Government Printing Office, 1993); and Paul Krugman, *Peddling Prosperity* (New York: Norton, 1994),

higher wages he or she can earn with more education. But we all benefit when children are well educated because there is less crime, less child abuse, more productive capacity, and so on. Consequently, public education is provided by local governments because a system of only private schools would lead to an underconsumption of education.

Water pollution is a good example of an external cost. For example, a paper mill might dump gallons of waste into a river. If this activity is unregulated, the people living downstream and along the river will bear many of the costs of paper production even though they may not be purchasing the products produced by the mill. The mill will ultimately overproduce because the total costs of its operations are not embodied in the cost of its product. Regulation, however, forces the firm to pay the costs of operating in an environmentally safe way and, as a result, reduces the production of the firm to a more efficient level.

Market Failure: Public Goods. **Public goods** cannot be purchased efficiently unless they are purchased by groups rather than by individuals. Public goods are indivisible among individual buyers. Additionally, once the good has been provided it is not possible to limit its consumption to those people who paid their share. For example, we cannot all individually purchase just the amount of national defense that we think we need. The "product" of national defense is indivisible. People who don't pay their fair share can't be excluded from enjoying the benefits of national defense. Consequently, as a society we must express our collective demand for a given level of national defense and then interact with our elected representatives to be sure they provide it.

Economic Stabilization. Imperfections in the market (e.g., inflexibility in wages and prices, inadequate economic information, etc.) are sources of economic instability that impose large costs on society. For example, when wages and prices fail to adjust adequately to changes in supply and demand for both workers and products, often joblessness will rise. Imperfect information increases the likelihood that people will make economic decisions that tend to retard economic growth. Many economists and policymakers contend that these problems justify a role for the federal government in economic stabilization.

Assessing the State of the Economy: The Business Cycle

Before we can determine the goals of economic policy, we must first agree on ways to measure current economic conditions. A doctor seeking to determine if a patient is sick will begin with the patient's vital signs (temperature, pulse, blood pressure, etc.). Likewise, policymakers attempting to assess the state of the economy tend to focus on key economic "vital signs."

The economy's position in the **business cycle** is the most obvious indicator of its economic health. Business cycles are commonly believed to be recurring periods of economic growth above or below the average (or trend rate) of economic growth. The average growth rate is different for different countries and can change over time for an individual country due to structural or demographic changes in the economy. The average growth rate for the United States during the post–World War II period has been just under 3 percent.[1] Figure 1.3 illustrates a hypothetical pattern of the business cycle. The vertical axis represents the

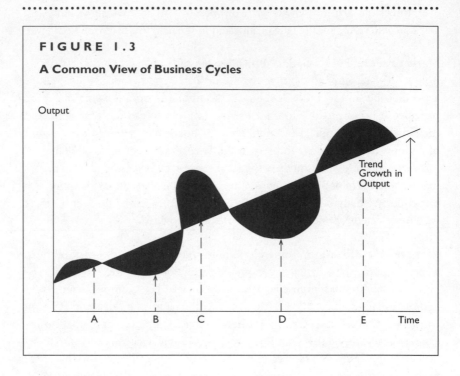

FIGURE 1.3

A Common View of Business Cycles

country's total output of goods and services; the horizontal axis represents time. The straight line represents the economy's trend rate of economic growth—that is, average or normal economic growth—and the line marking the boundary of the shaded areas represents actual levels of output at different points in time.

Business cycles are marked by turning points called **peaks** and **troughs.** Point A is the peak of an **expansion** phase of the business cycle. At points in time before A, economic activity was increasing. Economic expansions are characterized by high rates of job creation, rising income, greater production of output, increases in retail sales, and so on. To the right of point A the economy enters a period in which economic activity is declining. It continues to decline, below trend rates of growth, until it hits the trough at point B. This period of time between point A and point B is known as a **recession** or, alternatively, as a **contraction.** Recessions are characterized by increases in unemployment and business failures, reductions in output production, and falling income. A **depression** is an extremely severe recession. Between point B and point C the economy is growing again and is in the expansion phase of the business cycle.

Students are not alone in recognizing the complexities of economic policymaking. Reprinted by permission of KAL, Cartoonists & Writers Syndicate.

Business cycles are commonly measured from peak to peak, so all points between A and C represent one business cycle; points between C and E represent a second business cycle. Business cycles are characterized by their duration, which is the length of time between peaks. Additionally, business cycles are characterized by their severity, which is measured by the distance of the turning points from the trend rate of growth. Note that the second business cycle is of greater duration and severity than the first.

Table 1.1 lists expansions and recessions in the American economy since the end of World War II. Later in the chapter we will discuss the causes of, and potential responses to, the business cycle.

Assessing the State of the Economy: Measuring Unemployment

Unemployment is a key economic vital sign. The primary economic costs of unemployment are permanent losses in national output and income. When the economy fails to provide an adequate number of jobs for everyone who is *able*

TABLE 1.1

Postwar U.S. Economic Expansions and Recessions (year: month)

Recessions		Expansion	
Dates	*Length (months)*	*Dates*	*Length (months)*
1948:11–1949:10	11	1949:10–1953:7	45
1953:7–1954:5	10	1954:5–1957:8	39
1957:8–1958:4	8	1958:4–1960:4	24
1960:4–1961:2	10	1961:2–1969:12	106
1969:12–1970:11	11	1970:11–1973:11	36
1973:11–1975:3	16	1975:3–1980:1	58
1980:1–1980:7	6	1980:7–1981:7	12
1981:7–1982:11	16	1982:11–1990:7	92
1990:7–1991:3	8	1991:3–19??–?	?
(Average: 11 months)		*(Average: 52 months[a])*	

[a]Computed using data from expansions, excluding the current one.

Source: Thomas L. Wyrick, *The Economist's Handbook: A Research and Writing Guide* (St. Paul: West, 1994), p. A22.

and willing to work, actual production of goods and services falls well below potential production. People who could have been earning an income are not. No matter how much unemployment declines in the future, output and income lost today will never be made up.

The social costs of unemployment are high and include increased rates of suicide, domestic violence, and child abuse. Teenagers and members of minority groups experience higher rates of unemployment than the general population. For example, during 1992 the unemployment rate for people aged 16–19 was roughly three times the general unemployment rate. The unemployment rate for blacks was more than twice that for whites.

Whereas full employment is a generally agreed-upon macroeconomic goal, the concept of full employment is difficult to quantify. Intuition suggests that full employment means jobs for everyone in the labor force—100 percent employment. But most economists believe that a certain amount of unemployment is inevitable, perhaps even desirable. To understand why this is so, consider the different types of unemployment.

Frictional unemployment results when people with job skills are in the process of voluntarily switching jobs. Suppose you graduate from your college or university with highly valuable job skills and decide to begin your job search the day after graduation. First, you send out résumés. After several firms respond positively, you go on first and second interviews. Several weeks later job offers arrive and perhaps you take an additional two weeks to decide which offer to accept. During this entire time you are unemployed. But your unemployment is part of the normal process of looking for a desirable job. This frictional unemployment is not detrimental to you or society. On the contrary, it is beneficial because it promotes optimal job matching between employees and firms. Frictional unemployment tends to be short term and affects individuals with valuable job skills who are seeking to improve their quality of life through a better job.

Structural unemployment also results from the dynamic nature of a market-based economy but tends to be longer term than frictional unemployment and is usually involuntary. This type of unemployment usually results from a mismatch of skilled labor and job vacancies. The mismatch can be characterized in two ways: as a skills mismatch or as a geographical mismatch. In the first case, consider the move by businesses during the 1970s and early 1980s away from typewriters to computer-based word processing. Many skilled laborers who previously worked at building and repairing typewriters lost their jobs. At the same time, jobs were being created for people who could build and repair computers, as well as people who could write word-processing software. Because new skills take time to learn, periods of structural unemployment tend to occur whenever new technologies are adopted.

The geographical form of structural unemployment tends to occur when workers with job skills live in areas far away from job vacancies. For example, construction workers in Houston may be unemployed because of a glut of unoccupied housing and office space at the same time that construction job vacancies multiply in Salt Lake City. Why don't all the unemployed Houston construction workers just pack up and go to Salt Lake City? Because relocation is not always easy. Fear of the unknown, incomplete information, and inertia often prevent the geographic relocation that would reduce this form of structural unemployment.

Some government policies are meant to reduce structural unemployment or its impacts. For example, provisions in the federal tax code permit people to deduct from their taxable income all the costs of a job search and of moving to a new geographical area. Federally funded worker-retraining programs were established to assist workers who suffered job losses because of the North American Free Trade Agreement (NAFTA).

Cyclical unemployment results when the economy is in the recession phase of a business cycle. When output falls, firms need fewer employees to produce goods and services, and layoffs result. Cyclical unemployment is costly to society and is usually addressed by the federal government through economic stabilization policies. These policies (discussed later) represent attempts to reduce the severity and duration of recessions.

Because frictional and structural unemployment are natural occurrences in a growing economy, full employment has come to be defined as the absence of cyclical unemployment. Hence the "full employment" rate of unemployment is typically defined as the total amount of structural and frictional unemployment. This level of unemployment is more typically referred to as the **natural rate of unemployment.** The precise natural rate of unemployment is hard to quantify for many reasons, but economists generally believe that the natural rate of unemployment is about 6 percent, although there is a range of uncertainty around this number (Motley, 1994).

The (civilian) **unemployment rate** is measured as the percentage of people in the labor force who are both available for work and actively looking for work but unable to find a job. Unemployment in the United States is measured by the Bureau of Labor Statistics (BLS) in the Department of Labor. Each month employees of the BLS attempt to estimate the unemployment rate by surveying employers to count the number of payroll jobs and by surveying approximately 60,000 households from all fifty states and the District of Columbia to collect data on the labor-force activities of each adult in the household during the prior week. From these data the BLS computes civilian unemployment rates.[2] Figure 1.4 illustrates the U.S. record on unemployment from 1929 to 1994.

Assessing the State of the Economy: Measuring Output

One of the most important measures of the state of the economy is the amount of goods and services (i.e., output) being produced. All things being equal, a healthy economy is one that is able to produce increasing output over time. Stagnant or declining output means fewer choices for consumers, which makes them less able to satisfy their desires. In summer 1981, for example, Poland was experiencing an economic crisis. Limited quantities of goods and services were produced. In restaurants in Warsaw, diners would receive menus as they were seated only to be informed by their waiter that due to food shortages the

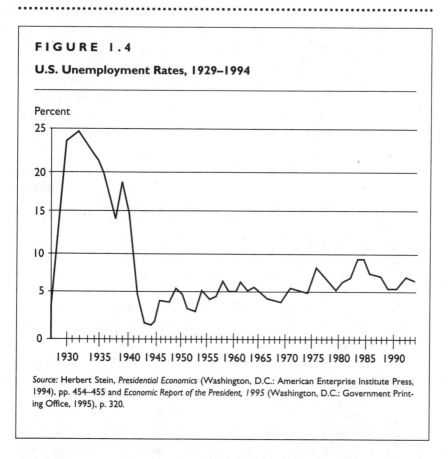

FIGURE 1.4

U.S. Unemployment Rates, 1929–1994

Percent

Source: Herbert Stein, *Presidential Economics* (Washington, D.C.: American Enterprise Institute Press, 1994), pp. 454–455 and *Economic Report of the President, 1995* (Washington, D.C.: Government Printing Office, 1995), p. 320.

restaurant was serving only one of the items listed. Additionally, the shelves in food stores were virtually empty and many other products were unavailable or in short supply. This forced Polish citizens to spend several hours daily waiting in long lines to purchase scarce amounts of food.

In order to track the amount of goods and services produced over time, the U.S. Department of Commerce computes, quarterly, a measure called the **gross domestic product** (GDP). GDP is the sum of the current purchase prices of all final goods and services produced in the domestic economy in a given time period (e.g., a quarter or a year).

It is important to clarify this definition. When we sum output produced we need a way to measure it all. Counting up the number of items produced wouldn't be useful because then we'd assign equal weight to a Harley Davidson motorcycle and a pair of Levi's. Instead, government statisticians multiply all goods and services produced by their purchase price and then sum the totals. For example, if 5,000 Harleys were manufactured and sold at a purchase price of $10,000 each, that would be $50 million of GDP. Gross domestic product is calculated using market prices (i.e., the purchase price) because these are an indicator of the value to society of each good or service.

Note that the definition of GDP refers to *final* goods and services. If you purchase a loaf of bread, only the price of the bread is counted in GDP. The price paid by the baker for flour, eggs, and milk is not included directly. To include intermediate goods in GDP would be a form of double counting because when setting the price of bread, the baker will incorporate the costs he or she pays for raw materials. To avoid double counting, the Department of Commerce also excludes the sale of used goods. So if you purchased used textbooks this year, their prices were not counted in GDP because they were already counted when they were originally produced.

Another key word in the GDP definition is *domestic*. We count in GDP only the goods and services produced within the geographic boundaries of the United States. The services of a Dutch surgeon operating in the United States count toward U.S. GDP. Cars produced at the Mercedez Benz factory in Alabama will also contribute to U.S. GDP. The legal services provided by a U.S. lawyer working in Tokyo will add to Japan's GDP, but not America's.

Total GDP in 1994 was $6.89 trillion. The broad expenditure categories used in this method of computing GDP include

- **Consumption,** defined as output purchased by people for use by themselves or another person. This is the largest component of GDP. It includes **durable goods** (e.g., cars, TVs, refrigerators), **nondurable goods** (e.g., shampoo, food, clothes) and **services** (e.g., overnight mail, legal fees, dry cleaning).
- **Investment,** defined as output purchased by the business sector (e.g., new vans purchased by Federal Express Corporation, new equipment purchased by Ben & Jerry's Ice Cream) plus expenditures on the purchase of new homes.
- **Government spending,** defined as federal, state, or local government purchases of goods and services (e.g., new pencils for members of Congress; new airplanes for the U.S. Air Force; expenditures on education; salaries of all federal, state, and local government employees).[3]
- **Net exports,** defined as goods and services produced in the United States and sold in foreign countries minus goods and services produced in foreign countries that are purchased by people living in the United States.

A problem with our current measure of GDP is that it increases as a result of increases in the *prices* of goods and services as well as increases in the production of goods and services. Suppose that total output is exactly the same in amount and composition this year as it was last year but that prices increased by 10 percent. Then this measure of GDP, also known as **nominal GDP,** will also increase by 10 percent. Examining only the raw data, we might conclude— wrongly—that the economy was growing robustly when, in fact, it wasn't growing at all. Government statisticians, therefore, also compute a measure of total output called **real GDP.** Real GDP is the sum of all final goods and services produced in the domestic economy in a given time period, but the purchase prices are computed on the basis of the value of the dollar in an agreed-upon year.

For example, we could compute real GDP for this year and last year by using the level of prices that prevailed in 1987. This yields a measure of GDP in *constant dollars,* one that zeros out the effects of inflation on our measure of total production because the "dollars" utilized in each year have the same purchasing power. If real GDP—that is, GDP measured in constant dollars—were to increase, it would be because there was an increase in production, not merely an increase in prices.

Assessing the State of the Economy: Measuring Inflation

Another important vital sign for the economy is the **inflation rate.** This is computed as the rate of change in the level of prices and is an indicator of whether purchased goods and services generally cost more, less, or the same over time. Inflation results when there is a mismatch between the amount of output society is able and willing to purchase (i.e., the aggregate amount demanded) and the aggregate amount of output that is supplied.

In order to better understand this national phenomenon, consider the following example. Suppose one of the students in your college or university is well connected and convinces the Rolling Stones to give a concert at your school. The concert is originally scheduled to take place in the basketball arena, which seats 5,000 students. Ticket prices are originally set at $20. But so many people want to see the Stones that one week before the concert tickets are being auctioned off for $75. In this case, demand far outstrips supply and prices are forced to rise.

Two possibilities exist for driving ticket prices down: increasing supply or reducing demand. For example, the student government could increase the supply of tickets by moving the concert to the football stadium, which seats 25,000. This massive increase in the supply of tickets would reduce prices. Or suppose the student government announced that due to unforeseen circumstances the Rolling Stones would still play, but Mick Jagger would not be able to perform. The dramatic decrease in demand following this announcement would reduce ticket prices back toward their original price of $20.

This example roughly illustrates how inflationary forces function at the national level. The cause of inflation is an excess of aggregate demand for output over the available aggregate supply of output. At the national level the only way to reduce inflation is to reduce total demand for output relative to supply. Hypothetically, inflation could be reduced by increasing the aggregate supply of output relative to demand. But the instruments of economic policy allow government to affect aggregate demand more deeply and more quickly. Government policies for changing aggregate supply operate indirectly and have their full effects only after many years.

To compute the inflation rate we must first have a measure of the aggregate price level. It's easy to go to the supermarket every week and see that the price of your favorite brand of soda stays constant at 98 cents for a two-liter bottle. Perhaps you also notice that the price of a one-pound bag of potato chips has increased 10 cents over the course of the semester, but the price of chocolate chip cookies and granola bars has dropped by 5 cents. How could you combine all this information to determine what is happening to prices in general? You could use a **price index** to calculate whether the aggregate price level is changing.

A price index is an average of the prices of a predetermined variety of products computed at specific points in time. A price index permits an easy comparison of the market prices of a collection of products in any given time period to their costs in other time periods.

A commonly used price index is the **consumer price index** (CPI). The CPI is an average of the prices of a hypothetical shopping cart filled with almost 400 goods and services typically purchased to meet the day-to-day needs of people in an urban household. This price index represents the government's attempt to measure the cost of maintaining a constant standard of living for an average family. For example, the CPI includes prices for cereal, macaroni, gasoline, movie tickets, rents, and mortgage payments, among others. In order to keep up with changes in consumer tastes, the government periodically surveys people to learn the typical purchases made by urban consumers. The contents of the hypothetical shopping cart are then adjusted accordingly.

In order to easily assess changes in prices, the CPI, like other price indices, is constructed to have a value of 100 in a given base period with prior or subsequent movements above or below 100 measuring changes in the overall level of prices. For example, in January 1993 the CPI was 142.6, indicating that a representative good that had cost $1 in 1982–1984 (the current base period) would cost $1.43 in January 1993.[4]

There are two types of price change that have not occurred in the United States in recent decades. The first is **deflation**, which happens when the average prices of goods and services decline over time. The United States has experienced many deflationary periods in its history. For example, between the end of 1929 and 1933, U.S. prices fell dramatically due to the Great Depression. The deflation rate, broadly measured, was just over 23 percent (i.e., an inflation rate of −23 percent). Even more uncommon in U.S. history is **hyperinflation**, which occurs when there are very rapid increases in the price level (i.e., every day prices increase). Hyperinflation is not defined in percentage terms but rather as an inflation rate so high that people are unwilling to hold cash because every day (or every hour) money is worth less and less in terms of the goods it will buy.

Inflation imposes a variety of costs on society, some of which tend to redistribute income from one group to another. In the case of the minimum wage, inflation during the 1980s redistributed income away from employees working for the minimum wage to their employers. Because the federal government has failed to increase the minimum wage by the same amount as inflation, employers paying the minimum wage in 1995 pay a lower real cost for labor inputs than they did a decade earlier. This illustrates a more general point regarding the costs of inflation: that people who must live on fixed incomes (e.g., retirees living on fixed pensions) or relatively fixed incomes (e.g., employees working under multiyear, fixed-wage contracts) lose purchasing power as a result of inflation. This helps explain why senior citizens often lobby heavily against economic policies that are likely to be inflationary.

To avoid the penalties imposed by inflation, many government benefit programs and a number of labor contracts include an automatic compensation for inflation called a **cost-of-living adjustment (COLA)**. For example, an employer might agree to annually increase wages based on last year's percentage increase in the CPI. In this case, wages do increase in response to increases in inflation, but with a delay.

Inflation is costly to society because it reduces business investment and expansion. A large source of the funds used by businesses to finance the purchase of new equipment or the building of new factories comes from individual savers via banks or other financial institutions. For example, when individuals buy new issues of Microsoft stock, they are providing financing for corporate expansion. But when inflation is high, many savers shift their savings into gold or other assets that tend to better preserve the purchasing power of their money. The result is less financing for business investment and less accumulation of productive **capital** (e.g., machines, factories). With less capital than would have accumulated without inflation, the economy will produce less.

Assessing the State of the Economy: The Level of Interest Rates

So far we have generalized about interest rates. But in the United States there is no such thing as "the" interest rate. Instead, there are many interest rates that have important effects on different segments of the economy. Some of the key interest rates and their significance are discussed here. The federal funds rate and the discount rate, two important interest rates determined by the Federal Reserve, are discussed in Chapter 3.

Among the most important interest rates are those paid out to purchasers of U.S. government bills, notes, and bonds. When the federal government borrows money to cover its budget deficits, it must pay interest on the funds it borrows. The U.S. Treasury does this principally by selling government securities on a regular basis throughout the year to a variety of investors, including individuals, pension funds, banks, and state and local governments. Investors pay the Treasury a specified sum that varies depending on the security purchased, and in return they receive interest plus subsequent repayment of their principal.

The Treasury sells two kinds of interest-earning securities: **marketable securities** and **nonmarketable securities.** Marketable securities are sold by the Treasury in what is known as a **primary market** and range in maturity from three months to thirty years. Marketable securities with maturities of one year or less are called **Treasury bills** (or T-bills). Securities with maturities greater than one year but equal to or less than ten years are called **Treasury notes;** securities with longer maturities are called **Treasury bonds.** These securities are marketable because the original purchaser doesn't have to keep them. Instead, at any time before the debt is repaid by the Treasury, an original purchaser may re-sell Treasury bills, bonds, or notes in a **secondary market** to anyone. In September 1993, 65.9 percent of U.S. interest-bearing public debt was in the form of marketable securities.

Nonmarketable securities are sold by the Treasury to individuals, foreign governments, and state and local governments. In this case the original owner must keep the security until the debt is repaid. If you have ever been given a U.S. savings bond on your birthday, high school graduation, or other important occasion, you are the owner of a U.S. government nonmarketable security. In September 1993, 34.1 percent of U.S. interest-bearing public debt was in the form of nonmarketable securities. Figure 1.5 indicates the distribution of interest-bearing debt in 1994.

Interest rates paid by the federal government on Treasury bills, notes, and bonds are important because they critically influence the interest rates that individuals and businesses pay for loans of similar length. Setting loan rates high enough to ensure a profit but low enough so that credit-worthy individuals and businesses will borrow money can be a tricky business. Interest rates on government securities have thus come to serve as a benchmark for private loans of similar length. For example, a bank issuing thirty-year mortgages to home buyers will use the interest rate on the thirty-year Treasury bond as a guide. In practice, private loans tend to be made at rates slightly higher than those charged the federal government for Treasury securities of a similar length. Banks and other sources of loanable funds consider the federal government to be a riskless borrower because, through its powers of taxation, the government can theoretically raise the money necessary to repay all its loans.

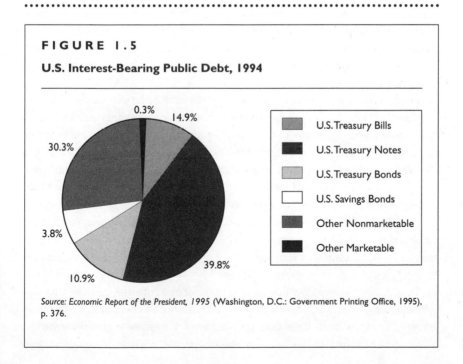

FIGURE 1.5

U.S. Interest-Bearing Public Debt, 1994

- U.S. Treasury Bills
- U.S. Treasury Notes
- U.S. Treasury Bonds
- U.S. Savings Bonds
- Other Nonmarketable
- Other Marketable

0.3%   14.9%   30.3%   3.8%   10.9%   39.8%

Source: *Economic Report of the President, 1995* (Washington, D.C.: Government Printing Office, 1995), p. 376.

Because individuals and businesses are much more likely to default on their loans, banks charge them a higher interest rate to compensate for the potential losses.

Another very important interest rate is the **prime rate.** The prime rate is the interest rate banks charge on loans to their best corporate customers. Business customers not so favored by the bank may receive loans at the prime rate plus 1 percent or the prime rate plus 2 percent, and so on. The prime rate serves as a benchmark for many loans to businesses. Not all banks will charge the same prime rate at the same time, but competition among banks tends to force some convergence to a single prime rate, much as four gas stations located at the four corners of a single intersection will tend to charge the same price for a gallon of gas.

So how could changes in the prime rate possibly affect you? Just as lower mortgage rates decrease the overall price of homes to consumers, lower prime rates will decrease the costs of expensive items that businesses must purchase. For example, suppose that Southwest Airlines is contemplating expanding its service by flying to six new cities on the East Coast. A senior executive determines that this expansion will require the purchase of twenty new airplanes from Boeing. Should Southwest go ahead with the expansion? This depends, among other things, on Boeing's selling price for the new airplanes plus the amount of interest Southwest Airlines will have to pay to borrow the money to purchase them. The lower the prime rate, the lower the cost of expansion, and the greater the likelihood that this move will be profitable and undertaken by Southwest.

Investments of this type by businesses tend to provide many new job opportunities. This helps to reduce the unemployment rate and increase real GDP. As large numbers of businesses in the economy expand in response to lower interest rates, workers find themselves with expanded job opportunities.[5] In this case, Boeing would need more employees to build the aircraft, and Southwest would eventually need to hire pilots, flight attendants, mechanics, and gate agents to staff and service the flights on the twenty new planes.

This can work in the opposite direction as well. A high prime rate tends to cause reductions in business investment and thus slower economic growth and fewer job opportunities. It is important to note that interest rates do not cause immediate changes in economic decisions because of the long lead time between a business decision to buy new equipment or a consumer decision to buy a house, car, or TV, for example, and the actual purchase and delivery of these goods. Therefore, increases in interest rates tend to precede economic contractions, and reductions in interest rates tend to precede economic expansions.

Assessing the State of the Economy: Deficits and Debt

The second presidential debate in Richmond, Virginia, was a dramatic event in the 1992 campaign. In a departure from traditional formats, the questioners in the debate were randomly selected, undecided voters from the Richmond area. A twenty-five-year-old woman, Marisa Hall, had heard much talk during the campaign about how the exploding national debt was harming the future economic prospects of the country, but she wanted to know what it meant for the individual. She asked the candidates, "How has the national debt personally affected each of your lives? And if it hasn't, how can you honestly find a cure for the economic problems of the common people if you have no experience in what's ailing them?" (Germond and Witcover, 1993: pp. 9–11).

Ross Perot responded that the seriousness of the problem had caused him "to disrupt my private life and business to get involved in this activity [running for president]. That's how much I care about it." He reflected that his upbringing in a family of modest means and his good fortune as an adult had led him to believe that he owed it to the country's children and his own children to do something about the sick economy.

President Bush was confused by the question. He said, "Obviously it has a lot to do with interest rates—"

The moderator interrupted, "She's saying 'You personally. You on a personal basis. How has it affected you . . . personally.' "

The president stammered further and then added, "Are you suggesting that if somebody has means, that the national debt doesn't affect them? . . . I'm not sure I get—help me with the question and I'll try to answer it."

Ms. Hall said, "Well, I've had friends that have been laid off from jobs. . . . I know people who cannot afford to pay the mortgage on their homes, their car payment. I have personal problems with the national debt. But how has it affected you, and if you have no experience in it, how can you help us, if you don't know what we're feeling?"

President Bush groped for an answer but never seemed to satisfy the questioner. Next, Bill Clinton responded that as governor of a small state he personally knew people hurt by economic conditions. He ascribed the mushrooming national debt to "twelve years of trickle down economics" and to "the grip of a failed economic theory [supply-side economics]." Clinton prescribed for the economy a program of more investment in jobs, education, and control of rising health care costs.

Marisa Hall asked an important question that night in Richmond. But we should recognize that a rising national debt is not necessarily a problem. President Thomas Jefferson questioned the wisdom of dramatically increasing the national debt in order to finance the Louisiana Purchase. In that case, the United States went into debt to finance the purchase of an investment that has paid for itself many times over. In your own life a comparative example might be going deeply into debt to finance four years of college. You would be making an investment in your own education that will more than pay for itself through better job opportunities and higher income.

A rising national debt is a problem when it is being amassed to finance increased consumption (rather than investment) and when it is growing faster than national income. In this case, public investments are not adequate to raise future income growth by an amount necessary to finance the debt. To better understand the problem, consider a college student who graduates and begins work at an annual salary of $30,000 a year. Suppose in the first year the student borrows $5,000 from Mastercard by running up a large balance to buy new suits and some furniture for his apartment. The following year the student gets a raise of $2,500, but he borrows $12,000 to buy a new car. The following year the student gets a raise of $3,000, but he borrows $25,000 to buy a condominium. If this graduate's debt continues to grow faster than his income, he will eventually be unable to pay all his monthly bills. The bank will repossess his car and home, and no creditor will lend him money for more purchases.

The problems posed for the federal government by a national debt growing faster than national income will be considered in Chapter 4. But first, let us understand the causes of the **national debt** and the federal **budget deficit** and the linkage between the two.

A budget deficit occurs when expenditures are greater than revenues; a **budget surplus** results from the opposite condition, when revenues exceed expenditures. The federal government has not experienced a budget surplus since fiscal year 1969.

Figure 1.6 illustrates changes in the federal government's nominal (not adjusted for inflation) budget deficit during the period from 1940 through 1994. Note that the budget deficit increased dramatically during World War II as outlays soared to finance the war effort. Large deficits are common in wartime as governments spare no expense for victory. Budget deficits also tend to increase when the economy is in a recession because outlays must increase to finance unemployment compensation and various welfare programs at the same time that tax revenues decline because fewer people are working and earning in-

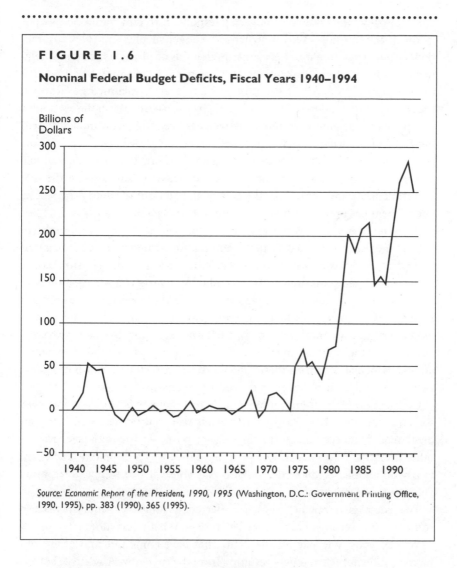

FIGURE 1.6

Nominal Federal Budget Deficits, Fiscal Years 1940–1994

Billions of
Dollars

Source: Economic Report of the President, 1990, 1995 (Washington, D.C.: Government Printing Office, 1990, 1995), pp. 383 (1990), 365 (1995).

come. This later source of increasing deficits has led policymakers to propose an additional measure of the federal deficit.

The **structural deficit** is a hypothetical concept that measures the expected size of the annual federal budget deficit *if* the unemployment rate during the year remained at the natural rate of unemployment (i.e., 6 percent). Thus, the structural deficit represents the *planned* components of government spending and tax policy rather than the budgetary response forced by the economy's position in the business cycle. A structural budget surplus indicates contractionary policy because it reflects either high levels of planned taxation or relatively low levels of government spending or both. A structural budget deficit reflects either low levels of taxation or high levels of planned government spending or both and is likely to have an expansionary effect on the economy.

A primary way to finance budget deficits has been to borrow money by selling Treasury securities. Every annual deficit is covered by borrowing; the borrowing places the country in debt; the debt accumulates. The U.S. national debt is an accumulation of all past budget deficits and surpluses of the U.S. government. At any given time, the debt is the amount of money the federal government has previously borrowed and not yet repaid.

If you buy a new four-year Treasury note this semester, the U.S. government will get the use of your $5,000 (the denomination of these Treasury notes) for four years. Every six months you will receive a check from the Treasury paying some of the interest due to you. At the end of four years you will get a final interest check plus your original $5,000. Maybe the government used your money to pay two month's salary for a government employee, or perhaps it was used to pay an environmental firm for toxic-waste cleanup. No matter what the expenditure, the government must fulfill its obligation to repay you your interest and principal. If, during these four years, the government continues to experience deficits, where will it get the money to repay you?

Consider examples from your own life here. What would you do if you owed someone money but your own income was still insufficient to pay off your debt? Would you consider borrowing money from one friend to pay back another friend? Would you consider getting a cash advance from one credit card to pay off another credit card? The only way you will ever be able to repay all your debts is if you begin to earn more than you spend.

The federal government is similarly affected. As long as expenditures exceed receipts, the government cannot reduce its debt. What it then does is to borrow some new money to pay off the debts that have come due and other new money to finance the new debt resulting from the current year's deficit. In reality, the only way that the federal government will be able to pay off the national debt is with budget surpluses. Reducing the budget deficit only ensures that the national debt will grow at a slower rate than it would have otherwise. As long as the annual budget runs a deficit, the national debt will not shrink.

Ironically, growing national debt also contributes to annual budget deficits. For example, at the end of fiscal year 1994 the federal debt stood at $4.64 trillion. To pay off the interest to owners of U.S. government securities, the federal

government needed to spend $203 billion. This is sometimes called debt ser-
vice; it appears in the federal budget as **net interest.** The total budget deficit for
fiscal 1994 was $203.2 billion; the $203 billion in net interest accounted for almost 100 percent of the deficit.

Think what this means. Had it not been for the cost of debt service on all the
budget deficits from previous years, the federal budget for FY 1994 would have
been very nearly balanced. In that sense, the debt feeds itself. The costs of paying off the debt contribute heavily to current annual deficits, which add further
to the debt.

Figure 1.7 shows changes in the total real national debt of the U.S. federal
government (i.e., in constant dollars). The national debt, adjusted for inflation,
increased substantially during World War II because of the large federal deficits
that resulted from the war. However, federal budget surpluses after the war
permitted a reduction in the amount of debt outstanding. The level of real debt

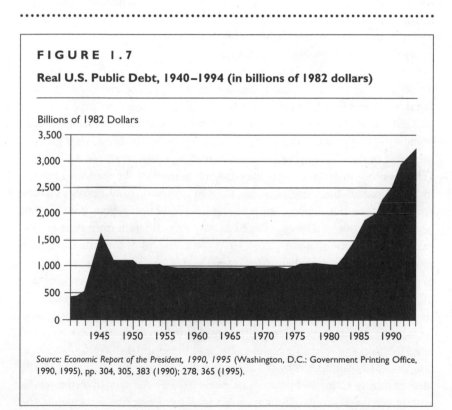

FIGURE 1.7

Real U.S. Public Debt, 1940–1994 (in billions of 1982 dollars)

Billions of 1982 Dollars

Source: Economic Report of the President, 1990, 1995 (Washington, D.C.: Government Printing Office,
1990, 1995), pp. 304, 305, 383 (1990); 278, 365 (1995).

then stayed fairly constant, although at a new higher level, until fiscal year 1982, the year President Reagan's first budget took effect. Note the increases in real debt that were due to the large budget deficits since 1982. The Budget Enforcement Act of 1990, enacted under President Bush, and the Omnibus Budget Reconciliation Act of 1993, enacted under President Clinton, imposed budgetary changes that increased various taxes and reduced spending on some government programs for a projected decrease in U.S. budget deficits of almost $1 trillion over eight years. But these changes will not turn the line in Figure 1.7 downward. They will only flatten the angle of the line's ascent.

The Role of Government in a Market Economy

Three macroeconomic theories currently dominate policy debates in the United States. Each of these theories views the interactions between employees, firms, and government somewhat differently. All three agree that the ultimate goal of policy is to promote macroeconomic stability, but they offer different policy prescriptions for pursuing that goal.

Politicians argue about these theories, but for practical reasons. When a theory seems to justify a particular policy direction, politicians grab onto it for political leverage. Liberal Democrats (and some Republicans) of the postwar period did this with Keynesian economics; Ronald Reagan did it with supply-side economics. In the former case, economic theory helped justify a larger government role in the economy; in the latter, a smaller government role.

Macroeconomists study how the component parts of the economy interact to influence variables such as unemployment, inflation, and output. But the economies we study are constantly changing. For example, your decisions on what goods to buy and what prices to pay are very different from your grandparents' or even your parents' decisions. If you are a typical consumer, you have more disposable income than your parents had at your age and a wider range of goods to choose from. Your decisions will also be affected by advertising you might see on TV or maybe by something you read about a product on an electronic bulletin board. Other major changes in our economy include the greater importance of international trade, the large number of women who have entered the paid workforce since the 1970s, and the gradual shift from an economy originally dominated by the agricultural sector to one dominated by the manufacturing sector and now to one dominated by the service sector. As the economy evolves, economic theory must change to describe it. However, the evolution of the economy tends to be gradual. Sometimes we experience periods when a model that used to characterize the economy quite well is giving way to a new model. During this time the theories of both models may appear to be correct for different sectors of the economy.

Another problem policymakers face in trying to identify the validity of a certain theory and its associated policy recommendations is that macroeconomics is not an experimental science. Imagine that you have a severe ear infection. The school doctor gives you two different antibiotics to take and a week later the infection is gone. What cured you? Was it the first antibiotic? The second antibiotic? The combination of the two? Or perhaps you got better in spite of the medication. Without more information, it's impossible to know. Likewise, so many different forces affect the economy simultaneously that policymakers always have a difficult time isolating the impacts of different economic policies and determining which policies are effective and which are not.

The lack of consensus regarding which macroeconomic theory is most reliable at any specific time complicates the formulation of economic policy. One of the major dilemmas of contemporary economic policymaking is this uncertainty and disagreement about the relationships among basic elements of the modern economy. Often we do not know which elements affect which others to what magnitude. Macroeconomic theory seeks to clarify those relationships. Therefore, it is important to have a rudimentary understanding of the major schools of economic thought in order to understand and actively engage in the policy debate.

Keynesian Economics

Keynesian economics is named for its originator, John Maynard Keynes, an economist who did some of his most significant work during the 1930s. Traditional Keynesian economics focuses on the short-run problems of the economy (especially unemployment) and thus on short-run policy solutions.[6] This is understandable because Keynesian theory was a reaction to the enormous economic misery brought about by the Great Depression. Few economists dispute that two forces ultimately determine the rate of inflation, the amount of output produced, and thus indirectly the unemployment rate. These two forces are the aggregate (i.e., total) supply of output and the aggregate demand for output.

But Keynes broke ranks with his predecessors and argued that because of frictions in labor markets and product markets, there was no tendency for full employment to prevail in the economy. On the contrary, he argued that these frictions created a tendency for the economy to wallow for long periods of time in recessions characterized by high rates of unemployment. During recessions, Keynes believed, these frictions caused a shortfall in aggregate demand relative to aggregate supply. Firms throughout the economy with plenty of goods to sell and very few purchasers would then respond by firing workers. The firms that manufactured goods would respond to reduced orders from the stores by firing workers. The unemployed workers would in turn reduce their purchases and aggregate demand would fall even further, setting off a vicious downward economic spiral.

Because Keynesians believe the principal macroeconomic problem is unemployment, policy focuses on its elimination. Keynesians contend that the *only* way to cure the massive unemployment and declines in production that result from recession is to use expansionary macroeconomic policy, to stimulate aggregate demand to a level sufficient to generate full employment. In this way, a deficiency in consumer and business demand for goods and services is offset by an expansion in the government's demand for goods and services. Because of the economy's tendency to stagnate in recession and because of the effectiveness of macroeconomic tools, Keynesians conclude that government has an essential responsibility to actively use its tools to stabilize the economy.

For example, Keynesian theory concludes that the Great Depression was finally ended when government expenditures on defense began to massively increase in anticipation of U.S. involvement in World War II. The government awarded millions of dollars in contracts to suppliers of ships, planes, tanks, guns, and ammunition. These firms then hired hundreds of thousands of workers to build war material. The newly employed defense-industry workers increased their purchases of goods and services, forcing other employers to hire more workers as well. Through this process an initial increase in government demand for output is believed to "prime the pump" and encourage a subsequent increase in consumption and business investment. Due to this Keynesian-identified **multiplier effect,** the resulting increase in output (and declines in unemployment) would be many times larger than the initial increase in government spending.

In order to finance an increased government demand for output, Keynesians traditionally recommended that taxes not be raised. Instead they proposed to borrow, by issuing Treasury securities, to finance rising deficits. Tax increases would actually diminish people's take-home pay and thus offset much of the increase in consumer and business demand that would follow the increases in government demand for output. Keynesians recognized that increased spending in the absence of increased taxes would lead to large increases in the size of short-run budget deficits, but they believed that once the economy had recovered sufficiently the president and Congress would be able to cut back on government spending, increase taxes, and therefore generate budget surpluses that could be used to reduce the debt. They assumed that government budget deficits and surpluses would essentially balance over the course of the business cycle, but they predicted no negative consequences if balance was not achieved. An additional benefit of this approach, according to Keynesians, was that the excess aggregate demand that caused inflation during major expansions could be offset by the tax increases and government spending cutbacks.

Keynesians believed that changes in tax policy and changes in monetary policy were weaker and less reliable macroeconomic tools than changes in government spending. For example, when government spending increases by $100, the entire sum is used for the purchase of new output. When individuals receive a $100 rebate in taxes, they are likely to spend only a fraction of the rebate, saving the rest. Aggregate demand will still increase, but not by as much as in the case of government spending.

The policy successes of Keynesian economics dominated the 1940s through the 1960s. Beginning in the late 1960s, however, the policy failures of Keynesian economics became more prominent. These failures appeared to result primarily from two factors: (1) the fallacy of certain critical assumptions in Keynesian theory and (2) an almost exclusive focus on only the short-run consequences of economic-policy decisions. Keynesians originally believed that as long as the unemployment rate was above the natural rate of unemployment, expansionary macroeconomic policy (e.g., an increase in government spending, a tax cut) would have no effect on the level of prices in the economy. Thus they falsely concluded that aggregate demand could be expanded right up to the point of full employment without causing inflation. In fact, this relationship is not as absolute as the early Keynesians believed. On the contrary, increases in aggregate demand may cause increases in inflation even when the economy is well below full employment.

Keynesians also originally believed that policies meant to increase or decrease aggregate demand for output would have neither short-run nor long-run effects on aggregate supply. But inflation, output, and unemployment are determined simultaneously by the relationship between aggregate demand and aggregate supply. For example, expansionary macroeconomic policy that seeks to increase demand for output while at the same time inadvertently reducing supply will result only in higher inflation with few or no changes in either output or unemployment.

During the 1960s, fiscal policy was very expansionary as a result of large tax cuts and huge increases in government spending to finance the war in Vietnam and the social welfare programs that were part of President Johnson's Great Society. As a result of these and other economic policies, inflation jumped from an average of 1.6 percent during the first half of the decade to an average of 3.8 percent for the second half of the 1960s. Because the higher inflation and higher interest rates that often result from overly expansionary fiscal policy tend to reduce business investment in new machines, the productivity of workers also tends to fall below what it could have been otherwise. Many economists believe that a legacy of the inflationary Keynesian policies of the 1960s was a major reduction in U.S. productivity beginning in the 1970s that caused downward pressure on the aggregate supply of output.

A third critical assumption that proved false was that policymakers could determine with a high degree of precision the potential output of the economy and how much unemployment was full employment. Additionally, it was believed that with the use of large-scale mathematical models of the economy, policymakers could determine exactly how big a federal budget deficit was needed to deliver the desired macroeconomic results. In reality, the economy has proven much more complex and quick to evolve than the early Keynesians predicted. Beginning in the 1970s, policy often failed to deliver the expected results.

John Maynard Keynes criticized policymakers who focused on the long run with his famous quote that in the long run we are all dead. But some forty years after publication of his most famous book, policymakers were forced to open their eyes to the fact that we were living in the long run and that the economy was suffering from their previously myopic views of economic policymaking. Specifically, the short-run focus led to policies that increased aggregate demand at the cost of higher inflation. This permitted actual output to approach (and sometimes even exceed) the full-employment level of output through the use of an "inflation surprise." The policy worked by keeping actual inflation above what most people expected. As a result, employees were willing to work for lower real wages than they would have if they had known the true inflation rate. Employers responded to the lower real wages by hiring more workers, and output rose while unemployment fell. But employees could not be fooled forever. During the 1970s workers became more aware of the impact of the "inflation surprise" on their purchasing power, and when they did, inflation lost most of its ability to generate lower levels of unemployment.

Monetarist Economics

Milton Friedman is often identified as the father of **monetarism,** but the theories of the monetarists were developed by many different economists, including Friedman. As a result, the term "monetarist" encompasses a large set of theories and policy conclusions not all of which are subscribed to by people who consider themselves to be monetarists. Nevertheless, the central ideas of monetarism tend to be diametrically opposed to those of traditional Keynesians.

Monetarists argue that the primary macroeconomic problem is not unemployment but inflation. With inflation in check, they contend, other macroeconomic goals become potentially achievable. Minimizing inflation must thus be the chief objective of macroeconomic policy, particularly monetary policy.

Recall that inflation results from an excess of total demand for output over total supply. Monetary policy that limits excessive growth in aggregate demand by limiting excessive growth in the money supply will consequently limit inflation. Although Friedman had been advocating this position since the 1950s, it did not begin to gain wide acceptance among policymakers until the 1970s, when the failures of traditional Keynesian theories regarding the existence of a permanent trade-off between inflation and unemployment became apparent.[7]

Unlike Keynesians, monetarists argue that the macroeconomy is inherently stable, and they believe that swings in the business cycle are due to erratic growth rates in the money supply. For example, monetarists tend to view the Great Depression as being primarily the result of the 30 percent *decline* in the money supply between 1929 and 1933 that was passively allowed by the Federal Reserve. This reduction in money substantially reduced aggregate demand and in turn caused deflation of 23 percent and a reduction in real GDP of 46 percent. Therefore, in the view of monetarists, inflation can be controlled and the severity of business cycles reduced through a policy of low and stable money-supply growth (Friedman and Schwartz, 1963).

Monetarists focus on the long run. They believe that attempts at fine-tuning the economy through the use of planned deficits to increase aggregate demand, output, and employment are ineffective at best and, at worst, counterproductive. Keynesians argued that an increase in the deficit would create a situation where government spending was higher relative to taxes, thus leaving individuals and businesses in a position to spend more. The monetarist counterargument is summarized by Milton Friedman's question, "Where do they think the money [to spend more] is coming from? The Tooth Fairy?" Friedman sees expansionary fiscal policy as the government giving people more money with one hand through government outlays or tax reductions while taking away an equal amount of money with the other hand through the process of borrowing to finance the resulting budget deficit (Stein, 1994: p. 287).

Monetarists argue that increased government spending or tax cuts **crowd out** private expenditures, leaving aggregate demand roughly unchanged. In the worst-case monetarist scenario, expansionary fiscal policy, financed through deficit spending, just increases current consumption while it crowds out business investment in new productive machines and factories. As a result, the economy's potential growth rate is lowered below what it could have been.

Since shortly after the appointment of Paul Volcker as chairman of the Federal Reserve Board in summer 1979, the Fed has apparently made control of inflation its primary goal. A rough measure of the Fed's success in this regard is that during the period 1970–1980 the average annual rate of inflation in the CPI was 11.2 percent, whereas during the period 1980–1990 the average inflation rate was 5.9 percent. But critics also noted that in the process of reducing the inflation rate from 11 percent in 1979 to 3 percent in 1983, monetary policy became so restrictive that the prime interest rate increased to 21.5 percent, the unemployment rate increased above 10 percent, and real GDP actually declined during 1980 and 1982.

In 1979 monetarism indicated that money-supply growth needed to be reined in to reduce inflation, but theory was not explicit as to how much and how quickly this should be done in order to limit the recessionary effects of the policy. Chairman Volcker was like a pilot flying the economy through thick fog with a compass but no map. He knew the direction in which he should head but was not sure if there was a mountain range blocking the course he had chosen.

By 1983 inflation had fallen to more acceptable levels and the economy was growing quickly. Between 1983 and 1989 the U.S. inflation rate averaged 2.5 percent per year. Unemployment continued to decline until 1989, when it was 5.3 percent, and the economy experienced the longest peacetime economic expansion on record. Even the recession of 1989–1991 was short and mild by historical standards. It seemed that the monetarists were correct: If only inflation were mastered, all other economic goals were achievable.

Supply-Side Economics

Supply-side economics was part of the economic counterrevolution against the theories and policy failures of traditional Keynesianism. A major spark for the development of supply-side theories was the dramatic decline in the productivity of U.S. workers that occurred after 1973. Specifically, from 1947 to 1973 U.S. workers on average were able to increase the amount of output they produced per hour by about 3 percent a year. This may not seem like very much, but at this rate of growth you could double the amount of output you produced in an hour in just twenty-four years. Rapid increases in productivity permitted higher real wages and standards of living for most U.S. workers during this time period.

From 1973 to 1979, however, output produced per hour increased at an average annual rate of only 0.8 percent. At that rate, U.S. workers would need eighty-seven years to double the amount of output produced, an indication that future generations are likely to enjoy much slower improvements in the standard of living (Stein, 1994: p. 219).

Those who were to become supply-siders began to ask questions about the source of the productivity slowdown and to wonder what could be done to restore high rates of economic growth. Unlike traditional Keynesians, supply-siders focus their analysis on the long-run development of the economy. Supply-side theories argue that the only sources of output growth (and thus new jobs) in the long run are (1) increasing labor-force participation or (2) greater labor productivity resulting from improvements in the quality of labor through better education or health care, improvements in technology, or increases in the amount of equipment utilized in production.

Labor-force participation can increase in a number of ways including immigration, demographic changes such as increased numbers of women working, elimination of mandatory retirement for older workers, or a willingness on the part of employees to work more hours. Supply-siders theorize that increases in the supply of workers tend to depress inflation-adjusted wages, which causes firms to be able and willing to hire more employees. With more people employed, output rises and the unemployment rate falls. It has been estimated that roughly one-third of U.S. economic growth between 1929 and 1982 was due to this (Denison, 1985: p. 15).

Increased productivity can reduce total employment in some firms and even some industries, but increased productivity will always, in the long run, lead to greater employment in the economy as a whole. For example, suppose you worked as a tailor or seamstress in a shop with three other people in a frontier town during the 1880s. You and two of your coworkers made shirts all day and did all the sewing by hand. Because it took so long to make a shirt, they were expensive and few people in town owned more than two shirts. Then one day the shop owner purchased a sewing machine and worker productivity soared. You could turn out six times as many shirts in a day as you used to. The shop owner responded by firing two of your coworkers. But because shirts could then be produced more quickly, their price fell, as did the price of all other clothes that could be made on a sewing machine. Falling prices eventually gave rise to an increased demand for clothes and stores to sell them. In the long run, factories that make clothes multiply, as do stores such as J. C. Penney and the Gap that sell them. Warehouses must be built and staffed to store clothes not yet shipped, and trucking firms spring up to move materials between factories and stores. Millions of jobs are created in the apparel industry that ultimately replace those that were lost in your shop. How many shirts do you own?

Education increases a worker's productivity by giving the individual an ability to do work of greater value and with greater proficiency. Better education has been estimated to be responsible for 14 percent of U.S. output growth between 1929 and 1982.

Increases in the amount of equipment in use also increase the amount of output a worker can produce. This is true in the manufacture of clothes, the production of agricultural output, and the number of tax returns an accountant can prepare. An estimated 19 percent of the increase in real output between 1929 and 1982 is due to increases in the amount of machinery used in production. Another factor related to this is technological change that includes new knowledge about how to more efficiently utilize machinery in the production process as well as new knowledge about how to manage firms more efficiently. This factor is estimated to be responsible for 28 percent of real growth during the 1929–1982 time period.

With the identification of key factors responsible for increasing output and employment, supply-siders examined Keynesian macroeconomic policies to determine how these key factors may have been affected. They concluded that the inflationary macroeconomic policies advocated by the Keynesians caused significant *reductions* in the amount of new machinery purchased by businesses and in the number of people willing to work. Supply-side theory also asserts that rising inflation promoted conditions that depressed savings. Banks and other lenders thus had a smaller pool of funds to loan, and fewer businesses were able to obtain the funds needed to finance the purchase of new equipment.

Supply-siders focus on increasing aggregate supply, in the long run, by targeting tax policy and, to a lesser extent, government spending to encourage equipment purchases by firms. Specifically, they propose reductions in corporate income tax rates, reductions or elimination of all taxes on savings, and tax advantages for firms investing in new machines. They also believe—in direct opposition to the Keynesian approach—in balancing the federal budget or at least keeping budget deficits to a minimum to avoid their retardant impacts on business investment.

Reductions in the rate of equipment purchases are also believed to have resulted from the enormous increases in government regulation that were part of public policy in the 1960s and 1970s. As businesses spent more money to comply with government regulations on workplace safety and pollution control, for example, they had less money available for investment. The costs of compliance also tend to reduce the profitability of potential equipment purchases, in some cases to the point where the purchases are no longer profitable. The recommended solution to this problem is to reduce government regulation.

Just as Kennedy and Johnson were the presidential champions of Keynesian economic policy, Ronald Reagan became the champion of supply-side economics. Reagan's initiatives included major reductions in personal and corporate income taxes, a reduction in the top individual tax rate from 70 percent to 50 percent, additional tax cuts to promote business investment, increased availability of individual retirement accounts (IRAs) to promote savings, and deregulation in many industrial sectors such as airlines and trucking.

The long-run macroeconomic impacts of these supply-side policies have been difficult to evaluate for several reasons, including the fact that they were first implemented during a severe recession when extraordinarily high interest rates were inhibiting business investment. A second problem is the short duration of the supply-side experiment. Due to the large deficits created by the Reagan tax cuts as well as problems in financing Social Security, taxes (e.g., Social Security taxes and excise taxes) were later raised significantly by Presidents Reagan, Bush, and Clinton. Another problem is that supply-side policies are targeted to affect the macroeconomy some ten or more years after their implementation. A truer test of supply-side policy than the economic performance of the United States during the 1980s would be its performance during the 1990s.

Proponents of supply-side economics point out that implementation of supply-side policy was followed by an economic expansion of record-breaking duration. Opponents of supply-side economics focus their attention on the large budget deficits that resulted from the enormous tax cuts of 1981 and the constraints that these deficits imposed on the economic programs of Presidents Bush and Clinton as well as the potential long-run costs of the deficits measured in terms of lower potential rates of economic growth.

The Role of Pragmatism in Economic Policymaking

The days of a completely passive governmental approach to economic policymaking are over. Whereas the debates over appropriate macroeconomic models and policy prescriptions are not a wasted exercise, policymakers are rarely free to substitute the dogmatic for the pragmatic. To paraphrase James Carville, one of President Clinton's chief political advisers during the 1992 campaign,

"When I make a mistake, someone just loses their election. When the administration makes a policy mistake, it can cause chaos throughout the entire country" (Woodward, 1994: p. 120).

Figure 1.8 illustrates how U.S. federal government expenditures, measured as a percent of the size of the economy, have changed since the start of the Great Depression. The federal government's claim to total output peaked during World War II, then fell by half. It rose again, slightly and briefly, during the Korean War. Since Keynesian macroeconomic theory became widely embraced in the 1960s, government expenditures have increased steadily and are now claiming roughly one-quarter of U.S. output.

The long-term increase in federal expenditures as a percent of GDP has occurred primarily for two reasons. First, the political process introduces an up-

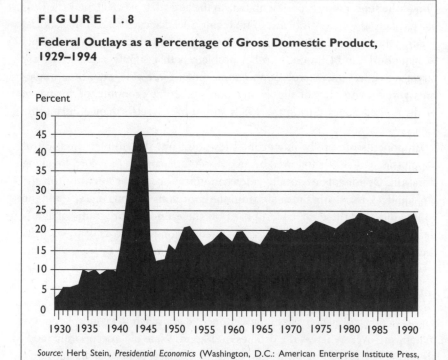

FIGURE 1.8

Federal Outlays as a Percentage of Gross Domestic Product, 1929–1994

Source: Herb Stein, *Presidential Economics* (Washington, D.C.: American Enterprise Institute Press, 1994) pp. 452–453; and *Economic Report of the President, 1995* (Washington, D.C.: Government Printing Office, 1995) pp. 274, 365.

ward spending bias because once a federal benefits program has been created it quickly gains a constituency of voters and members of Congress who will fight relentlessly to avoid cuts in spending. New programs are continuously introduced as new social and economic needs are recognized, but old programs almost never die.

A second problem results from the growing size of mandatory government outlays, particularly the entitlement programs created during the 1930s and 1960s. As the size of the population grows, more and more people become eligible for federally insured savings deposits, Social Security, Medicare, and so on. Without changes in the enabling legislation that establishes the standard benefit packages, these programs will continue to become even more expensive. But as Congress has learned repeatedly, reducing the size of the benefit packages provided by the entitlement programs is politically difficult, if not in some cases politically suicidal. Figure 1.9 captures the scope of this problem by illustrating how the size of mandatory outlays has grown as a percent of federal expenditures.

Because the federal government has come to control the disposition of such a large percentage of our total output of goods and services, its policy decisions will have far-reaching impacts on all of the people within the country and millions of people abroad. Some of those impacts will be unexpected and undesired, as the following case illustrates.

In November 1991 President Bush, aware that credit-card interest rates in the range of 18–20 percent were acting like a drag chute on economic growth, commented, "I'd frankly like to see the credit-card rates down. I believe that would help stimulate the consumer and get the consumer confidence moving again." The following day Senator Alfonse D'Amato (R–N.Y.) introduced an amendment to pending legislation that would have capped the interest rates banks charge on their credit cards at the rate the IRS charges delinquent taxpayers plus 4 percent. At that time the amendment would have set a cap of 14 percent on credit-card interest rates, a significant reduction. The legislation passed in the Senate by a vote of 79 to 14 (Pae, 1991: pp. A3–A4).

Major banks argued that the high rates were needed to cover losses caused by delinquents and responded to the Senate vote by threatening to issue credit cards only to the least risky customers and deny credit cards to everyone else. This move, banks insisted, was necessary to prevent losses that would occur with lower credit-card rates. It also would result in the cancellation of the credit cards of *half* of all the Americans who held them. The measure never passed the House and was never implemented. President Bush's attempt to make credit more available and thus stimulate the economy actually started a

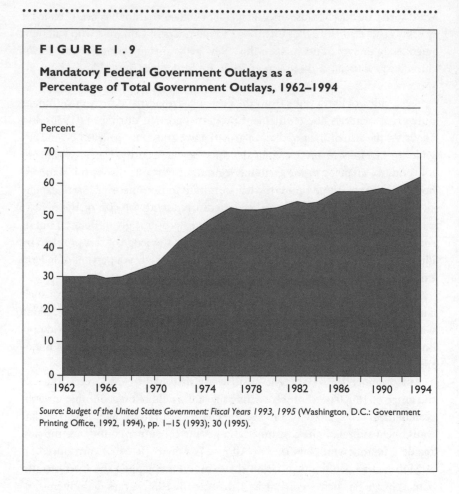

FIGURE 1.9

**Mandatory Federal Government Outlays as a
Percentage of Total Government Outlays, 1962–1994**

Source: *Budget of the United States Government: Fiscal Years 1993, 1995* (Washington, D.C.: Government
Printing Office, 1992, 1994), pp. 1–15 (1993); 30 (1995).

chain of events that ultimately would have severely reduced credit availability.
It was emblematic of the dilemma all presidents face in trying to direct so complex a national economy.

Conclusion

A carpenter trying to build a house wouldn't be of much use without knowledge of how to use a hammer, nails, saw, level, and other tools of the trade.
Likewise, economic-policy analysis conducted without an understanding of
fundamental economic principles rarely yields useful results. Especially impor-

tant in conducting economic analysis is the ability to strip away the misleading effects of inflation by converting nominal variables into real variables. Then, for example, we don't look at a doubling of nominal wages and assume incorrectly that people's purchasing power has doubled as well.

The U.S. economy alternates between periods of recession and expansion, sometimes minor and sometimes severe. There are several measures of economic vitality: rates of growth in real output approximately equal to the long-run average, stable prices, unemployment rates roughly equal to the sum of structural and frictional unemployment, long-term real interest rates that are low enough to encourage business investment in new equipment, but not so low that they will promote inflation.

Economic stabilization is conducted through countercyclical macroeconomic policy that limits the severity of both expansion and recession phases of the business cycle to keep the economy on a sustainable path of moderate economic growth. Among the potential tools available for achieving this goal is fiscal policy, characterized by changes in either government spending or taxes. The nature of fiscal policy is determined jointly by the President and Congress through the passage of appropriations (spending) or tax bills. An expansionary fiscal policy would incorporate increases in government spending or tax cuts or both; a contractionary fiscal policy would incorporate decreases in government spending or tax increases or both.

Annual federal budget deficits are financed by federal government borrowing and are the source of increases in the national debt. Projections for smaller deficits only indicate that the national debt should begin to grow at a slower rate than it did during the 1980s. But the only way to actually reduce the size of the debt is for the government to collect revenues in excess of outlays.

Monetary policy is also a potential tool for economic stabilization. In this case, changes in the growth rate of the money supply affect total demand for output either directly through changes in people's spending habits or indirectly through the conduit of interest rates.

Although countercyclical macroeconomic policy is the generally agreed-upon goal of the federal government, economic policymakers tend to disagree about the causes of economic problems and the exact means by which goals should be achieved. Traditional Keynesians view unemployment as the most serious macroeconomic problem and urge the active use of expansionary macroeconomic policy, especially fiscal policy, to stimulate the economy. Keynesian policy analysis focuses on short-run economic problems and solutions.

Monetarists consider inflation to be the country's primary economic problem, arguing that other goals are more difficult to achieve when inflation is high. They recommend use of monetary policy, as necessary, to limit growth in aggregate demand and thus inflation. Monetarists focus more on the long-run consequences of policy than traditional Keynesians.

Supply-siders believe that the long-run rate of economic growth, measured as real output growth, should be the primary concern of macroeconomic policy. Unlike monetarists and Keynesians, they don't focus on the direct effects that monetary policy and fiscal policy have on aggregate demand for output. Instead they focus on the indirect effects of these policy tools on the aggregate supply of output. Supply-side policy emphasizes using fiscal and monetary policy to create an environment characterized by stable prices, little regulation, and tax incentives that will encourage businesses to purchase new equipment and develop new and more efficient means of production. Additionally, supply-siders believe that disincentives to work, particularly in the form of high personal income tax rates, should be kept to a minimum.

2

....

Development of
the Modern Political
Economy

Money is a singular thing. It ranks with love as man's
greatest source of joy. And with death as his greatest
source of anxiety. Over all history it has oppressed
nearly all people in one of two ways: either it has been
abundant and very unreliable, or reliable and very
scarce.

—John Kenneth Galbraith

●●

IMAGINE YOURSELF A young entrepreneur setting up a leather-harness business in 1880. You've learned the trade of harness making from a master and now you want to go out on your own to make a living from the booming horse-accessory business. So what does it take to start and run your own business?

Not very much, as it turns out. There aren't many banks, and none that are willing to supply you with capital. So you take your savings and a little money you borrow from relatives and the profit you made from selling off that parcel of land your father-in-law gave you when you were married. You build an addition to your barn and hire a few local boys to do the tanning of hides and the cutting and stitching. You purchase a small ad in the county newspaper, and you take some of your saddles and bridles to the local market to sell.

If you are diligent, your business begins to grow. More people want to buy your harnesses, so you enlarge your building and hire more help. You take enough money out of the earnings of the business to pay your help a few dollars a week and to care for your family. Everything else you earn gets plowed back into the business.

Years go by, and business is booming. As the population grows, more people have more horses than ever before. Demand for your harnesses and saddles is steady. You keep hiring more people and building more space to keep up with the demand. You are now producing so many saddles and harnesses that disposing of the waste products from your tanning and cutting activities becomes a problem. So you build a sluiceway from your factory to the stream a few hundred yards away and flush the industrial wastes into the stream, where they are carried away.

As you hire more workers they begin to complain to each other about their long hours, low wages, and dangerous working conditions. You don't think you can make an adequate profit if you pay them more or shorten their hours or spend money on safety improvements that don't make manufacturing more efficient. So you turn down their demands and tell them that if they don't like their jobs with you they can quit and work elsewhere, that there are plenty of people you can hire who would be happy to have their jobs.

The 1890s roll around and with them two things that threaten your business—and your future—very dramatically. First is a national financial depression, the panic of 1893, that causes bank closures, business failures, and widespread unemployment. People don't have the money they once did to buy your saddles and harnesses. Demand slows, profits vanish, and you have to lay off workers and cut back production. At the same time, strange new inventions called motor cars are beginning to appear on the dusty roads of America. Nobody sees these cars as anything but an indulgent luxury at first, but there do seem to be more of them around all the time.

Your business never recovers. There is no relief from the shrinking demand you suffered in the depression. You earned too little to pay back the money you'd borrowed for your last expansion. Nobody wants to lend you more money because the future of the horse-accessory business is not very promising; the future is automobiles, not horses.

By the end of the 1890s, your business is dead. You are carrying debts that will hang over your head for the rest of your life. All of your employees have been cast into unemployment and had no benefits of any kind, no pension accumulation, and no source of relief during the time it took them to find new work. Like many entrepreneurs of your time, you are the victim of the relentless business cycle and of the accelerating pace of change in a country where new technologies are bringing great opportunities but also great risks to the marketplace.

Think about the vignette you just read. Anything missing? Those of us who live in the last decade of the twentieth century ought to have quickly noted that in the last decade of the nineteenth century, the federal government was completely absent from this tale. When our entrepreneur sought to set up his business, he needed no permits or approvals from the government. There were no government agencies to lend him start-up funds at subsidized interest rates, to help train his workers, to give him favorable tax breaks to ease his early years in business—in part because he owed no taxes.

No laws regulated his relations with his workers. He alone determined the hours they worked, their wages, and their working conditions. They had no right to a minimum wage, to a maximum number of hours, to a safe workplace, or to collective bargaining. Our entrepreneur paid no workers' compensation or unemployment insurance or Social Security taxes. When he had to deal with his industrial wastes, he did so in the easiest and least costly way: He dumped them into a nearby stream. There were no laws to prevent him from doing this; no permit was required.

By the same token, when the business began to fail, there was no cushion for the owner or the employees. There were no government programs to provide relief from the depression or to encourage development of new markets or worker retraining when the company's principal product line became obsolete. When the business failed, there were no bankruptcy laws to provide the owner with a graceful exit. There was no unemployment insurance or pension-guarantee program or subsidized health care for the unemployed workers. Everyone—owner and employees—had to fend entirely for themselves.

Prevailing economic doctrine and political belief of the time held that the government was to be a very minor player in the national economy. It would build some roads and canals, establish tariffs to raise its own revenues, coin money, deliver the mails, and not much else. That was the doctrine of laissez-faire: economic enterprise should be left to the workings of the free market.

In the late nineteenth century, most of the economy was unregulated, the federal budget was almost always balanced or producing a surplus, individuals and corporations paid no direct taxes, and most Americans asked and expected little from government. Most, in fact, lived their lives with little or no direct contact of any kind with the national government except for the use of its currency and its post office.

That, of course, produced real economic freedom. But it was a peculiar kind of economic freedom, and for many Americans it was a freedom fraught with risks and dangers. Income distribution was very uneven. Labor had no rights and workers toiled for low wages over long hours under dangerous conditions. A few very large and powerful businesses dominated the government and ensured that it acted—when it acted at all—in their best interests. The business cycle fluctuated widely from boom to bust. Many Americans lived lives of great personal insecurity, unprotected from the uncontrollable forces of the weather, the market, and the workplace. The economic freedom that Americans cherished in theory served some Americans better than others.

The economic history of the twentieth century is about the changing relationship between the government and the national economy. In the collapsed perspective of comparison between the last decades of the nineteenth century and the last decade of the twentieth, the changes seem dramatic, even radical. But those changes unfolded gradually and fitfully over many decades. Many were the product of political and economic battles that went on for years.

The central dynamic—and the central dilemma—in this century of change was the tension between the desire for economic freedom and the desire for economic security. A market free of government was a market full of risks. But a market free of risk was a market full of constraint. Americans in the twentieth century sought to find the right balance between freedom and regulation, between a private economy and a powerful government. In this chapter, we examine some of the critical episodes in this changing relationship and the kind of political economy they have yielded at the end of the twentieth century.

The Populists and the Progressives

The forty years following the Civil War were a period of rapid and dramatic change for the United States. The population grew from 35 million to 76 million. The growing population spread rapidly westward; by 1890, a leading historian of the time declared the end of the frontier. More American people meant more and larger markets for American businesses; the economy expanded and changed.

The modern American economy took root during this period, and its development was driven by the coincidence of several factors. One was a scarcity of labor and the resultant demand for mechanization of agricultural and industrial production. This demand stimulated American inventors to dizzying heights of creativity, as Table 2.1 indicates.

To harness this burgeoning economy, a new form of economic enterprise began to emerge: the corporation. These were unique entities whose capital was divided into shares of common stock. Shares could be held by a single individual, a family, a small group of investors, or they could be bought and sold openly in a **stock market.** New capital could be raised through a public sale of stock in a corporation. Risks could be spread over many shareholders. And people who lacked the skills or interest to start their own businesses could

---

TABLE 2.1

Selected New Inventions, 1867–1900

Dynamite (1867)	Adding machine (1884)
Typewriter (1873)	Automobile (1885)
Internal combustion engine (1876)	Cotton picker (1889)
Telephone (1876)	Diesel engine (1892)
Reinforced concrete (1877)	Refrigeration (1895)
Electric lights (1878)	Motion pictures (1895)
Electricity-generating station (1882)	Wireless telegraph (1895)
Steam turbine (1884)	Sound recording (1898)

participate in the economy—and reap its fruits—by buying stock in public corporations.

As corporations grew in size, they became more complex. The tasks of managing the corporation were divided by functions: production, advertising, sales, personnel, facilities, and management. Corporate management came to be regarded as something of a science, and the founding of the Wharton School of Finance at the University of Pennsylvania in 1881 marked the beginning of the movement to train professional corporate managers.

The age of invention and the emergence of the corporation coincided with important developments in communications and transportation. A national infrastructure expanded rapidly after the Civil War as telegraph wires laced the countryside and railroad tracks began to link every community with every other. By the end of the century, telephones were becoming more common and automobiles began to appear. The Wright brothers got an airplane to fly in 1903, and airplanes were soon carrying mail. In 1888, a couple of Chicago entrepreneurs dreamed up the idea of selling goods all over the country by publishing a catalog and shipping products by mail. Their young company, Sears and Roebuck, was soon in competition with every local business in America.

The growing complexity of the national infrastructure encouraged the development of national markets. A farmer who raised cattle in Texas could sell them in Chicago. Guns manufactured in Hartford could be sold in Wyoming. Burgeoning corporations competed intensely to sell more oil, operate more railroads, manufacture more steel, or produce more tobacco. Local and regional businesses, some of which had once enjoyed local monopolies, soon found themselves competing with much larger and more powerful national organizations called **trusts.** A trust was a group of corporations in the same industry who operated as a unit to reduce the costs of competition. The most successful of these were the Standard Oil, cotton oil, whiskey, sugar, and lead smelting trusts.[1]

Local businesses responded to the competition from national trusts in primarily two ways. Some simply capitulated and sold out to, or merged with, the trusts. Intrastate railroads, unable to compete with Union Pacific, sold it their track and rolling stock. Local oil drillers sold their wells to Standard Oil. Some smaller companies simply went bankrupt—the victims of a ferocious competition they could not survive.

The other reaction was to seek government protection. In the decades after the Civil War, as the economic marketplace grew in size and scope, many Americans came to feel victimized by large economic forces that had permeated their economy and, increasingly, their government. To secure their place in this new economy, these Americans sought government intervention to ensure open competition and prevent unfair practices. As historian Frederick Jackson Turner wrote, a philosophical turnaround was taking place: "The defences of the pioneer democrat began to turn from free land to legislation, from the ideal of individualism to the ideal of social control through regulation by law" (Turner, 1920: p. 277).

The first notable impact of this movement was the Interstate Commerce Act of 1887, which created the first independent regulatory commission, the Interstate Commerce Commission (ICC). The act required railroad rates to be "reasonable and just"; prohibited unfair practices such as pooling, rebates, and rate discrimination; and outlawed charging higher rates for short hauls than for long hauls over the same rail line. Three years later, Congress enacted the Sherman Antitrust Act, which declared illegal every contract, combination, or conspiracy in restraint of trade and made it a crime to monopolize trade among the states or with foreign countries.[2]

These two laws were more significant for the effect they had in initiating a pattern of government involvement in the economy than for any major changes they made in the marketplace. By the mid-1890s, the demand for even more government intervention had been accelerated by the Populist movement. The **Populists** were largely agrarian by occupation and angry by disposition. At their national convention in Omaha in 1892, they made their case.

> Our country finds itself confronted by conditions for which there is no precedent in the history of the world; our annual agricultural productions amount to billions of dollars in value, which must, within a few weeks or months, be exchanged for billions of dollars of commodities consumed in their production; the existing currency supply is wholly inadequate to make this exchange; the results are falling prices, the formation of combines and rings, the impoverishment of the producing class. We pledge ourselves, if given power, we will labor to correct these evils by wise and reasonable legislation, in accordance with the terms of our platform. We believe that the powers of government—in other words, of the people— should be expanded . . . as rapidly and as far as the good sense of an intelligent people and the teachings of experience shall justify, to the end that oppression, injustice, and poverty shall eventually cease in the land.

The Populists had some political impact on local elections in the Midwest and the South, but they and their leader, William Jennings Bryan, were soon melded into the Democratic Party. Bryan was the Democratic nominee for president in 1896, but he lost to Republican William McKinley. Bryan's failure kept much of the Populist agenda from immediate enactment, but reform proposals never die as quickly as the movements that spur them. When the reform banner was picked up by the Progressives after the turn of the century, much of the Populist legacy was carried forward.

The **Progressive movement** grew from different roots than did the Populists: more middle class than blue collar, more urban than rural. But like the Populists, the Progressives sought to wrest control of politics and the economy from a narrow and powerful elite. They found champions in Teddy Roosevelt and later in Woodrow Wilson. Progressivism had a potent impact as well in state and municipal governments. By the time the Progressive era came to a close on America's entry into World War I, a major reshaping had begun of the relationship between the government and the economy.

- The trusts had been regulated and new protections had been created for competition in the marketplace.
- Farmers and workers had begun to organize to use the instruments of government authority to gain a larger share of national wealth.
- The federal government had begun to regulate the manufacture and sale of food and drugs.
- Business domination of politics had been reduced—though hardly eliminated—by the establishment of direct primaries, which took the power to nominate candidates away from the sole control of the political bosses. The direct election of U.S. senators resulting from the Seventeenth Amendment (1913) had a similar effect.
- Government efforts to stabilize credit, interest rates, and banking practices had begun with the Federal Reserve Act of 1913.
- The Federal Trade Commission Act (1914) and the Clayton Antitrust Act (1914) sought to stiffen federal prohibitions on unfair trade practices and restraints on competition.
- Several measures were passed by Congress (but soon struck down by the courts) to regulate working conditions, hours, and child-labor practices in interstate commerce.
- To meet federal revenue needs in a more predictable way, a personal income tax was created with the ratification in 1913 of the Sixteenth Amendment. In the early years, only incomes greater than $5,000 were taxed and rates were below 1 percent on incomes under $25,000. In 1914, only 358,000 Americans paid federal income tax. But this new revenue source would grow to much greater prominence in the years that followed.

By the time the nation's attention turned to the war that was raging in Europe, America had become the world's largest and most homogeneous market and the world leader in industrial production. From a population of 31 million in 1860, America had grown to a nation of 92 million by 1910. America's gross domestic product had more than quintupled. The number of people engaged in production had grown from about 10 million to over 35 million, and national income had grown from $6 billion to nearly $30 billion.[3] American farmers grew 254 million bushels of wheat in 1870, 897 million bushels in 1914 (George, 1982: p. 111). Crude-oil output increased from 2.5 million barrels in 1865 to 266 million barrels in 1914 (George, 1982: p. 21).

And as the American economy grew in size and complexity, the federal government became a larger participant in economic activities. In 1880, the government role was minuscule. By 1917, government was much more deeply involved in the regulation of manufacturing and commerce, in determining banking practices, and in controlling credit. The age of corporate capitalism was well under way, and it was growing increasingly clear that government would play a major role in shaping its development.

World War I, Normalcy, and the Great Depression

Wars often have significant and lasting effects on social and economic life. World War I illustrates clearly why this is so. In this war 4.7 million Americans served in uniform. Of these, 2.8 million were drafted in what was only the second and by far the largest military draft in American history. During the war, the federal budget grew from $713 million to $18.5 billion. Dozens of new agencies sprang up to manage the war effort: the Council of National Defense, the War Industries Board, the War Shipping Board, and the Food Administration, to name just a few. Citizens' freedoms were restricted in ways that would not have been tolerated in peacetime. Federal government propaganda mills, led by the Committee on Public Information, ground away around the clock.

Great wars are won by economies as well as armies. The availability and reliability of equipment, arms, and food weigh as heavily as bravery and tactical cleverness in determining victory. To win World War I, the federal government intervened heavily and directly in the American economy. It became a major purchaser of goods, and its orders caused new businesses to spring up and old ones to change their product lines. American soldiers abroad were given the highest priority on the beef and grain raised by American farmers at home. The sale of war bonds deeply affected the financial markets.

The end of the war did not bring a complete cessation of the governmental energies it generated. The federal budget remained significantly larger than it had been before the war. To better manage the federal government's enlarged budgetary responsibilities, Congress enacted the Budget and Accounting Act of 1921. This law created the Bureau of the Budget to help the president prepare an annual budget recommendation, and it created the General Accounting Office to help Congress audit the agencies of the government.

For all the upheaval it wrought in the national economy, World War I brought about no major revisions of prevailing economic doctrine. Government intervention expanded in minor ways during the 1920s—the Federal Radio Commission was established to assign frequencies to radio stations, for example; the Federal Power Commission was created to oversee water projects; and the federal government began to regulate the stockyards where cattle were prepared for slaughter. But the prewar consensus, that the economy functioned most efficiently with minimal government intervention, remained largely in place through the 1920s. Government interventions were piecemeal and narrowly targeted. They were not motivated by any economic theory that offered a real challenge to traditional economic liberalism. As countries abroad began to experiment with socialism and fascism—that is, with highly planned and centralized economies—most Americans reacted with revulsion. If anything, the economic centralization emerging in parts of Europe caused American leaders to be even more defensive about and protective of the free market economy. "The American system," Herbert Hoover wrote,

> has gone further toward solutions of economic security of the individual than any other system of society. . . . Fascism has made improvements in Italy, but at an immeasurable cost of human liberty . . . and we stand in brilliant contrast with the drab failure of the Socialist system of production as we see it at work in its great Socialist exemplar, Russia. Our system of liberty—through its stimulation of competitive individual effort, the creation of enterprise, its development of skill, and its discoveries in science and invention which come from intellectual freedom . . . secured the production of the greatest quantities of commodities and services and in the most infinite variety known in the history of man. (Hoover, 1934: pp. 38, 42)

The postwar period that President Warren Harding had called "normalcy," and the economic ideas that sustained it, all came a cropper on the dark Tuesday in October 1929 when the stock market crashed. The value of stocks had risen steadily during the 1920s. The prosperity of growing numbers of American investors rose with them. Further, investors were aided by speculative practices that allowed them to purchase stock "on margin," that is, without putting up the full cost of each share. For many Americans with money to invest, stockholding had become an important form of wealth—wealth that seemed to grow with dizzying speed in the 1920s. The Standard and Poor's Index, measuring the value of common stocks, grew from 6.86 in 1921 to 26.02 in 1929.

When the bottom fell out of the stock market, the booming American economy of the 1920s quickly went into reverse. The value of common stocks dropped in less than a year to what it had been in 1921. In six weeks in fall 1929, the value of a share of AT&T fell from $336 to $197, of General Motors from $182 to $36, of Montgomery Ward from $467 to $49, and of Union Carbide from $414 to $59 (Campagna, 1985: p. 68). Real GDP (measured in constant 1982 dollars) declined from $704.6 billion in 1929 to $496.1 billion in 1933—a nearly 50 percent decline in the value of American goods and services (*Economic Report of the President, 1990*).

The stock market crash was not the sole cause of the depression, but it set off a series of explosions that blew out the weak points throughout the economy. American farmers had struggled for much of the decade as stable or falling prices and steady or shrinking markets made it hard to pay off the loans they had taken out to pay for tractors, trucks, and other new equipment to make them more efficient. Tariff policies designed to protect farmers also made it harder to expand markets abroad for American agricultural products. The agrarian economy was in a precarious state before the stock market crash; it quickly collapsed after it.

The banking system was another disaster waiting to happen. There were almost 30,000 American banks in the early 1920s, most of them small and operating only in one state. Many, in fact, had only one office. Banks were in fierce competition, subject to little effective regulation, and closely tied to local or regional economies. State-chartered banks were not obligated to become part of the Federal Reserve System, and many failed to follow prudent banking practices. In the 1920s, a number of these banks joined in the speculative investing of the period.

A growing economy had masked the dangers of these banking practices, but the stock market crash brought them into full view. Banks began losing money as local economies collapsed and borrowers defaulted on their loans. Americans who lost money by investing in margin accounts went to the banks to draw out savings to pay off their loans. But many banks did not have enough money in reserve to meet these withdrawal demands. This produced in some places a bank panic. Bank deposits were not insured, and depositors rushed to withdraw their funds before banks ran out of money. Some didn't get there in time. Banks closed down: 659 of them in 1929, 1,352 in 1930, 2,294 in 1931 (Leuchtenberg, 1958: p. 256). Thousands of Americans lost their savings—and their faith in the banking system.

The stock market crash was followed by years of economic decline. The whole capitalist world seemed plague-stricken. American industrial production declined in all sectors. In 1929, 4.5 million cars were sold; by 1932, car sales had dropped to 1.1 million (Kemp, 1990: p. 66). Overall industrial production measured by the Federal Reserve index dropped from 110 in 1929 to 91 in 1930 to 58 in 1937. Wholesale prices dropped by a third from 1929 to 1932. National income declined from $83.3 billion in 1929 to $40 billion in 1932. With the economy in a tailspin, millions of Americans were thrown out of work. By the end of 1932, 23.6 percent of the workforce—nearly 12 million people—were out of work.

In the despair produced by these economic calamities, Americans grew increasingly desperate for help—and hope. As the depression deepened and lengthened, faith in the self-righting capabilities of the economy began to recede. President Herbert Hoover counseled patience. "The fundamental business of the country, that is, production and distribution is on a sound and prosperous basis," he told the country's citizens (Lyons, 1964: p. 217). But optimism faded quickly, and Hoover felt compelled to initiate some government actions to cope with the depression. He encouraged cities and states to increase their spending on relief and public works. He solicited promises of increased capital investment from utilities and railroads. With Congress, he took measures to stabilize agricultural production. In 1931, Hoover proposed the creation of a Reconstruction Finance Corporation with authority to loan funds to private entities for projects that would create new jobs.

But the depression persisted and worsened over the course of Hoover's term. Americans were finding it increasingly hard to believe that the American economy had the capacity to fix itself. For a growing number, faith in capitalism began to erode. More and more, the hungry and unemployed began to look to the federal government to rescue them from the effects of the depression. There was little in the economic theory or political history of the United States to justify significant government intervention in the economy. But in the dark days of the depression, practical needs pushed history and theory to the bursting point—and opened the floodgates for a sea change in the relationship between government and the economy in America.

The New Deal

Franklin Roosevelt is a pivotal figure in American economic history. But he was not a trained economist, nor was he especially interested in economic theory.

He was a pragmatic politician: a former progressive legislator in New York, assistant secretary of the navy during World War I, Democratic candidate for vice president in 1920, and governor of New York when the depression set in. In the 1932 election, he offered the American people no unique or fully articulated economic theory. He only promised to try new approaches until he found something that worked. "The country demands bold, persistent experimentation," he said. "It is common sense to take a method and try it. If it fails, admit it frankly and try another. But above all, try something."[4]

When Roosevelt took office in 1933, the experimentation began. In the years that followed, much of the edifice of the modern political economy was constructed. It is important to remember, however, that this was an awkward, evolutionary process. New Deal initiatives were pragmatic and often disconnected from one another. Some worked, some didn't. Some were permanent, some only temporary. Some were later deemed unconstitutional. The long-term effects of the New Deal are enormous, but its impact was more the residue of trial and error than the implementation of a consensual economic theory.

The New Deal affected many aspects of the American economy, the most important of which were these:

- The federal government began to manage the national agricultural system. A new Farm Credit Administration became a major source of credit for American farmers. Broad-scale programs were established to improve farming practices and conserve valuable soil. A program of price supports and production quotas was put into effect to maintain agricultural price stability.
- The federal government broadened regulation to stabilize the banking and securities industries. The Federal Deposit Insurance Corporation was established to insure bank deposits and restore faith in the banking system. The Securities and Exchange Commission was created to regulate the stock markets and prevent the excesses that permitted the crash of 1929.
- Broad federal protection was granted to workers and organized labor. The Norris-LaGuardia Act affirmed the right of workers to join labor unions. The National Labor Relations Act went further, creating a National Labor Relations Board to protect workers in organizing unions and to assist in collective bargaining. The Fair Labor Standards Act created the first federal minimum wage and the forty-hour workweek with time and a half for overtime.

- The first broad-scale federal entitlement program, the Social Security system, was created. This provided a government-guaranteed pension for retired workers who had contributed through payroll taxes to a national trust fund.
- The microeconomic impact of the federal government spread to a number of new markets and industries with the creation or expansion of independent regulatory commissions such as the Federal Communications Commission and the Civil Aeronautics Board.

More important than the individual impacts of any of these, however, was their combined impact in changing American expectations about the government role in the economy. Franklin Roosevelt had plenty of political enemies. There were many Americans who thought him a dangerous radical bent on destroying economic liberty. But to a much larger number of Americans, for example, the 61 percent of the electorate who voted for his reelection in 1936, he was a prophet of hope. To most of them, Roosevelt had demonstrated that the economy could not be left to regulate itself, that capitalism could survive only if government was empowered to give it the direction it could not provide for itself and to curb its natural excesses.

As Americans set about the task of repairing their torn economy, some American economists took careful note of a new book, *The General Theory of Employment, Interest, and Money* (1936), by an English economist named John Maynard Keynes. Keynes and his adherents—Keynesians, as they came to be called—were not offering some mere exceptions to classical economic theory; they were arguing instead that laissez-faire was an untenable theory for guiding a modern industrial economy. Keynes suggested not merely that government intervention was a necessary evil in hard times but that the government should regularly use its full force to weigh in against cyclical pressures in the economy. Some American policymakers began to see Keynes's arguments as a theoretical explanation or justification for growing government intervention in the American economy.

Franklin Roosevelt and the other New Dealers were not Keynesians. That is, they were not driven by any broadly conceptualized view of the proper relationship between the government and the economy. They were politicians who wanted to serve the people who elected them by coping with the worst economic crisis in American history. But their actions seemed to offer some dramatic evidence that maybe Keynes was on to something. Maybe modern economies need not be left alone by government. Maybe, in fact, fiscal policy could be seen as a mechanism for directing the economy to accomplish politically desirable objectives such as higher employment or lower inflation. By the 1940s, the combination of Keynesian theories and New Deal policies had begun to dramatically alter American expectations about the relationship between government and the economy.

World War II

In many ways, World War II had as large and enduring an effect as the New Deal in establishing the modern political economy. American participation in World War II supercharged the economic recovery that the New Deal had barely begun. The war provided something that the New Deal did not: enormous demand. Indeed it provided the greatest demand for goods and services in American history to that point. To fight the largest war ever, the government needed soldiers and sailors, more than 16 million before the war was won. It also needed tanks, planes, ships, food, and weapons. Industrial production exploded and jobs multiplied rapidly. The GDP more than doubled between 1940 and 1945, and corporate profits increased by 50 percent (Campagna, 1985: p. 187; *Economic Report of the President, 1986*). Twelve million people were unemployed in 1932, only 670,000 in 1944.

Much of the material needed to fight the war was in short supply: rubber for tires, meat for soldier's meals, gasoline, steel. To ensure that military needs for these materials had first priority, a system of national rationing and distribution was established. Prices and wages were also brought under government control to limit the inflation that such surges in demand tend to produce. These programs added up to the most intense economic regulation in American history, and, surprisingly perhaps, they generated very little significant political opposition. Americans more willingly surrendered their economic freedom than at any other time in history.

Government expanded to unprecedented proportions during World War II, and federal government expenditures obliterated historical precedents. In 1939, total federal expenditures were $8.8 billion. By 1945, they had reached $92.7 billion. To pay its bills, the federal government raised taxes to higher levels than ever before. Americans filed 7.5 million personal income tax returns in 1939; by 1945, 50 million tax returns were filed. To get its revenues sooner, the federal government imposed payroll deductions in 1943, a practice that has remained in effect ever since. And the federal government borrowed money on a scale unprecedented in history. During the period from 1941 through 1945, the federal government accumulated deficits of $169 billion. The national debt went from $48.2 billion in 1939 to $271 billion in 1946.

Individual Americans were affected by World War II in equally dramatic ways. Personal income spiraled upward during the war. Real per capita personal income more than doubled between 1940 and 1945. To replace men who had gone off to war, women entered the workforce in larger numbers than ever before, often in jobs that had previously been regarded as too demanding for women. The expansion of industrial activity took place primarily in the North and the West. It encouraged one of the great population migrations in human history: the movement of black Americans from the rural South to the industrial North in search of jobs in wartime industries.

Then toward the end of World War II, a grateful nation sought ways to reward the veterans who had borne the burden of the fighting. In 1944, Congress passed the GI Bill of Rights. Among the provisions of this bill were two that changed the face of American society and the American economy. One was the creation of subsidies for veterans to attend college. The GI Bill supported veterans and their families while they were getting college degrees. This created unprecedented access to higher education in America. Before World War II, college had been largely the preserve of the wealthy. In the late 1930s, only 7 to 8 percent of Americans between the ages of eighteen and twenty-four attended college; only 143,000 bachelors degrees were awarded in 1936. After the war, veterans poured into America's colleges. In 1950, 497,000 bachelors degrees were awarded. The GI Bill permitted many Americans for whom college would never have been an option to get a college degree.

The GI Bill also subsidized the purchase of homes for veterans. It provided guarantees for the mortgage loans they took out from banks. If the veteran failed to pay off the mortgage, the government would ensure that the bank did not lose money. This greatly reduced the risk for banks in lending money to veterans and opened the door to home ownership to many Americans whose families had never owned their own homes. After the veterans came home from the war, the countryside was quickly abloom with new housing construction. From 1946 through 1956, the Veterans' Administration guaranteed almost 39 million new mortgages. In 1940, only 44 percent of Americans owned the homes in which they lived. By 1970 the percentage had grown to 63. World War II and the GI Bill converted a nation of renters into a nation of homeowners.

America at the end of World War II was a different country from the one that had entered the depression in 1929. But no change was more remarkable than the alteration that had occurred in the relationship between the federal government and the American economy. The modern political economy had undergone rapid maturation during this period. By the end of World War II, few Americans expected or wanted a return to the days of laissez-faire. The political agenda was filled with questions about the economic role of the government, but they were questions about the scope of that role, not whether there should be one. A mixed economy—part private, part public—had come of age. When the war ended and many Americans wondered how the economy could absorb all the returning veterans, few doubted that the federal government would play a leading part in finding the answer.

Government and the Postwar Economy

Two primary tasks faced America's political leaders after World War II. One was to prevent the domestic economy from slipping back into its prewar doldrums. The other was to define America's role in international affairs.

Activity on both those fronts began even before the war was over. The GI Bill is one example of that. So, too, was the Bretton Woods Conference in New Hampshire in 1944. Here representatives of the capitalist nations met to set up a system of fixed exchange rates for international currency and to establish an International Monetary Fund from which these countries could borrow. In 1945 in San Francisco, another international conference created the United Nations as a forum for the countries of the world to work out their disagreements peacefully.

The domestic economy was the major concern of national policymakers in the immediate aftermath of the war. The need for government leadership was widely assumed. In 1946, Congress passed the Employment Act, which declared more clearly than ever before the extent of the government's obligation to direct the economy: "The Congress hereby declares that it is the continuing policy and responsibility of the Federal Government to use all practicable means consistent with its needs and obligations and other essential considerations of national policy, with the assistance and cooperation of industry, agriculture, labor, and state and local governments, to coordinate and utilize all its plans, functions and resources ... to promote maximum employment, production and purchasing power."

When Republicans regained control of Congress in the 1946 elections, for the first time since 1930 they had an opportunity to reverse the momentum that the New Deal and the war had generated in politicizing the economy. It is notable that except in the area of federal protection of the rights of labor unions, they reversed very little.

In 1948, Americans reelected Harry Truman, a Democrat, and returned the Democrats to the control of Congress. Through his administration and those that followed, whether Republican or Democratic, government and the economy became more deeply intertwined. Dwight Eisenhower, who served as president from 1953 through 1960, was no fan of the New Deal or of big government. Yet during his administration, the federal government established the Small Business Administration to aid small businesses, began construction on a massive federal highway system, developed the St. Lawrence Seaway, and initiated an intensive space-exploration program.

During Eisenhower's presidency, federal expenditures grew by 30 percent. Five of Eisenhower's eight budgets included a deficit. And when the economy went into a deep recession in 1958, Eisenhower sought to use fiscal policy to encourage a recovery. Though a genuine fiscal conservative, Eisenhower could not turn back the clock. Government had become a central participant in economic policymaking.

New technologies—nuclear power, genetic engineering, wonder drugs, herbicides and pesticides—also generated demands for government regulation. The emergence of a genuine global economy with research, production, marketing, and sales rapidly spreading across national boundaries required increasing government attention to trade and tariff policy. A series of shocks in the international energy market forced government to respond with new energy policies and new agencies to implement them. The welfare state began to grow in America as elsewhere after World War II, and a growing portion of the American population found itself reliant on government programs for economic support to meet daily needs for food, shelter, and medical care.

And in the twenty-five years that followed World War II, the American economy grew dramatically. This produced great benefits for the American people—directly through steadily rising incomes and indirectly through a broadening array of tax-supported government programs to enhance their economic security. As the economy grew, so did the willingness of American politicians to create new programs to benefit the American people. Government spending grew faster as the economy grew faster, as Figure 2.1 indicates. By 1995 federal spending had grown to 22 percent of GDP. Compare that with 1929, when federal expenditures were 3 percent of GDP, to get a sense of the way the government role in the economy has grown.

As America settled into the postwar period, Keynes's ideas took firmer hold than ever before. Franklin Roosevelt had justified massive government intervention in the economy as a largely temporary measure for dealing with the "emergency" of the depression. He made little theoretical claim that government

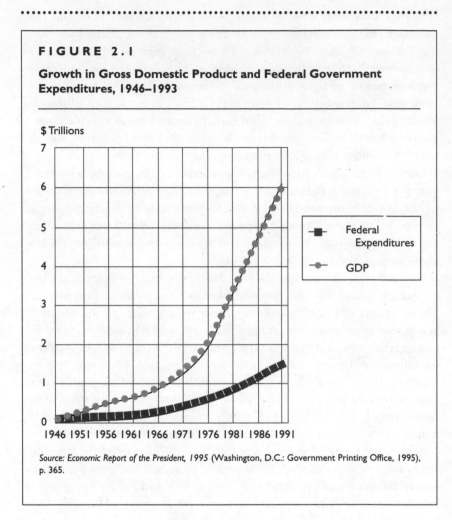

FIGURE 2.1

Growth in Gross Domestic Product and Federal Government Expenditures, 1946–1993

$ Trillions

| Federal |
| Expenditures |
| GDP |

1946 1951 1956 1961 1966 1971 1976 1981 1986 1991

Source: Economic Report of the President, 1995 (Washington, D.C.: Government Printing Office, 1995), p. 365.

ought to become a permanent part of the national economy, only that the need to overcome the depression and then to win the war required a sizable dose of government intervention. The Employment Act of 1946 and other postwar measures began to firm up the assumption of permanent government intervention, but it was not until the Kennedy administration that an American president was willing to admit that fiscal policy—government decisions about spending and taxes—ought to be consciously used to influence private economic activity.

Kennedy and most of his economic advisers believed in countercyclical fiscal policy—increase government spending or lower taxes to stimulate the economy; decrease spending or raise taxes to slow it down. In that sense, he was the first avowedly Keynesian president. But he realized he had to convince the American people, and many members of Congress, that spending, budget deficits, and inflation were not necessarily sins if they were part of a strategic effort to stimulate economic expansion.

Keynesianism took hold firmly in the 1960s and early 1970s. More often than ever before, the federal government ran annual budget deficits—not simply because it miscalculated or because revenues fell short of projections but often because it consciously sought to spend more than it collected in revenues in order to stimulate economic activity. The government budget became more than just an accounting device used to balance spending and revenues. It became as well a principal tool for directing national economic activity, and the federal government became increasingly comfortable with its use. Even the Republican president Richard Nixon declared, "Now I am a Keynesian."

The Reaction to the New Political Economy

The deeper the government penetrated the American economy, the more it was held accountable for economic failures and shortcomings. Businesses complained about the high costs of complying with government regulation. Presidential candidates were defeated when their party presided over a sluggish economy: Nixon in 1960, Gerald Ford in 1976, Jimmy Carter in 1980, and George Bush in 1992. Americans everywhere complained about taxes, high interest rates, and unemployment.

By the mid-1970s, the intensity of government intervention and Keynesian theory were under attack. To many Americans, the economy seemed stifled by too much regulation, and government had grown too large, too invasive, and too costly. The most common symbol of the apparent barrenness of economic policy was the surge in federal budget deficits and the growing federal debt that resulted. The government in Washington seemed congenitally unable to balance its own budget.

The long postwar boom had ended. The vast industrial capacity built up by high rates of investment began to exceed consumer demand. This tended to depress rates of profit, which discouraged new investment. Prices continued to rise in spite of this, creating a new phenomenon in the American economy that economists called **stagflation**—high unemployment, inflation, and slow economic growth. The Keynesians had no good explanation for this, and economic theories as well as economic policies were thrown into confusion.

A serious recession occurred in 1974–1975. But it was different from previous downturns in the business cycle. Prices did not fall and the dollar continued a long-term decline in purchasing power. When the economy began to recover, many plants that had closed during the recession did not reopen. The heavy industry on which the country had depended for decades went into decline, and companies lost market share to foreign competitors or moved their own manufacturing facilities abroad to take advantage of lower wage and regulatory costs. At the same time, high-tech industries and the service sector (fast food, computer programming, health care, education, etc.) began to boom.

As the bloom fell from the Keynesian rose, a school of economists known as the monetarists became more prominent. The intellectual leader of the group was Milton Friedman of the University of Chicago. The monetarists believed that stability in the economy could best be achieved through control of the money supply rather than through adjustments of government spending and taxing, through monetary policy rather than fiscal policy. To the monetarists, the key federal agency was the Federal Reserve Board, which had the power to increase or decrease the money supply to affect interest rates and economic growth. Monetarists also believed that the interventions of the federal government into the economy—particularly through regulatory policies—should be reduced to unleash the forces of the free market.

By the mid-1970s, action was under way to deregulate some aspects of the economy. Price regulations were lifted on natural gas. Regulation of commercial airlines, which had included assigning routes and setting fares, would significantly diminish by the mid-1980s. The Civil Aeronautics Board, a federal agency that had regulated the airlines since 1938, went out of business. Many restrictions on banking were removed in 1980.

In his campaign for the presidency in 1980, Ronald Reagan proposed a substantial cut in federal income taxes to stimulate economic activity. Reagan had become a proponent of what was known as supply-side economics.

Supply-siders, led by economist Arthur Laffer, believed that the principal problem facing the American economy was its punitive tax structure, which discouraged investment and production. A sizable cut in tax rates, they believed, would leave more money in the hands of individuals and corporations. The savings rate would also rise, giving financial institutions more money to lend. Investment would thus grow, leading to economic expansion and increased employment. The federal budget deficit would not increase substantially, despite the tax cut, because lower tax rates applied to higher incomes and more workers would keep revenues in balance with government expenditures. Or so the supply-siders contended.

Reagan's version of supply-side economics, which some called Reaganomics, was composed of large personal and corporate income tax cuts, increases in military expenditures, and decreases in social welfare spending. Congress followed Reagan's lead and passed the Economic Recovery Tax Act and the Budget Reconciliation Act in 1981. Nondefense outlays were cut by $31 billion, individual income tax rates were cut by 25 percent over three years, the capital-gains tax was reduced, and special provision was made for tax-deferred individual retirement accounts, or IRAs.

Much of Reaganomics was based on a good deal of wishful thinking, as even some Reagan aides later admitted. David Stockman, Reagan's budget director in 1981, told a reporter that "none of us really understands what's going on with all these numbers" (Greider, 1981: p. 38). Output and employment did not expand fully enough or rapidly enough to compensate for the budget deficits caused by the 1981 tax cuts.

Later in the Reagan administration, inflation declined and some sectors of the economy boomed. But by the end of the Reagan years, the annual budget deficit was up to $152 billion. Federal debt had risen from $940.5 billion to

All three major candidates in the 1992 presidential election were concerned about a weak economy. They differed significantly, however, in their diagnoses and prescriptions. Reprinted by permission of Steve Kelley and Copley News Service.

$2,707.3 billion during Reagan's presidency. An important consequence of this was the sense of real constraint that fell on Reagan's successors. George Bush said in his 1989 inaugural address, "We have more will than wallet," meaning we can't afford many of the programs we'd like to undertake.

When Bill Clinton came to the White House in 1993, one of his first major efforts was an economic recovery program that sought, through a mixture of tax increases and spending cuts, to reduce the federal deficit over five years. Clinton's proposals barely passed Congress in August 1993. The effects of that program, coinciding with a national economic recovery, led to a significant reduction in the size of the federal deficit in fiscal year 1994. New trade agreements were also approved during the early part of Clinton's term. But other Clinton policy initiatives, notably in health care and welfare reform, were unsuccessful in the 103d Congress. In 1994, confronting a now familiar reality, Clinton appointed a special commission to seek ways to reduce the budget impacts of spending on mandatory entitlement programs.

The 1994 congressional elections raised anew the old questions about the proper government role in the economy. For the first time in forty years, Republicans took control of both houses of Congress. Most of the House Republicans had pledged to support a Contract with America (see Box 2.1), a document that challenged many prevailing practices—and some underlying theories—of government intervention in the economy. The Contract promised action to secure a balanced-budget amendment to the Constitution, a steep reduction in economic regulation of business, and deep cuts in federal spending. The 1994 election signaled clearly that the central economic dilemma of the twentieth century—the effort to balance economic freedom and economic security—was still unsettled.

Change and Its Outcomes

Contrast today's entrepreneur with the one we encountered at the beginning of this chapter. An individual starting her own business today would probably begin by reviewing available government programs to help finance new enterprise and provide tax subsidies for start-up companies. The business might locate in a local industrial park where utilities, roads, and other essential services are available at low cost. The contemporary entrepreneur would need to get a permit to manufacture goods and another one to sell them. Federal, state, and local tax forms would have to be prepared, and the new business would probably be incorporated under the laws of the state in which it was located.

· ·

BOX 2.1

Republican Contract with America, 1994

This year's election offers the chance, after four decades of one-party control, to bring to the House a new majority that will transform the way Congress works. That historic change would be the end of government that is too big, too intrusive, and too easy with the public's money. It can be the beginning of a Congress that respects the values and shares the faith of the American family.

Like Lincoln, our first Republican president, we intend to act "with firmness in the right, as God gives us to see the right." To restore accountability to Congress. To end its cycle of scandal and disgrace. To make us all proud again of the way free people govern themselves.

On the first day of the 104th Congress, the new Republican majority will immediately pass the following major reforms, aimed at restoring the faith and trust of the American people in their government:

First, require all laws that apply to the rest of the country also apply equally to the Congress;

Second, select a major, independent auditing firm to conduct a comprehensive audit of Congress for waste, fraud or abuse;

Third, cut the number of House committees, and cut committee staff by one-third;

Fourth, limit the terms of all committee chairs;

Fifth, ban the casting of proxy votes in committee;

Sixth, require committee meetings to be open to the public;

Seventh, require a three-fifths majority vote to pass a tax increase;

Eighth, guarantee an honest accounting of our Federal Budget by implementing zero base-line budgeting.

Thereafter, within the first 100 days of the 104th Congress, we shall bring to the House Floor the following bills, each to be given full and open debate, each to be given a clear and fair vote and each to be immediately available this day for public inspection and scrutiny.

1. The Fiscal Responsibility Act

A balanced budget/tax limitation amendment and a legislative line-item veto to restore fiscal responsibility to an out-of-control Congress, requiring them to live under the same budget constraints as families and businesses.

2. The Taking Back Our Streets Act

An anti-crime package including stronger truth-in-sentencing, "good faith" exclusionary rule exemptions, effective death penalty provisions, and cuts in social spending from this summer's "crime" bill to fund prison construction and additional law enforcement to keep people secure in their neighborhoods and kids safe in their schools.

3. The Personal Responsibility Act

Discourage illegitimacy and teen pregnancy by prohibiting welfare to minor mothers and denying increased AFDC for additional children while on welfare, cut spending for welfare programs, and enact a tough two-years-and-out provision with work requirements to promote individual responsibility.

4. The Family Reinforcement Act

Child support enforcement, tax incentives for adoption, strengthening rights of parents in their children's education, stronger child pornography laws, and an elderly dependent care tax credit to reinforce the central role of families in American society.

5. The American Dream Restoration Act

A $500 per child tax credit, begin repeal of the marriage tax penalty, and creation of American Dream Savings Accounts to provide middle-class tax relief.

6. The National Security Restoration Act

No U.S. troops under U.N. command and restoration of the essential parts of our national security funding to strengthen our national defense and maintain our credibility around the world.

7. The Senior Citizens Fairness Act

Raise the Social Security earnings limit which currently forces seniors out of the work force, repeal the 1993 tax hikes on Social Security benefits and provide tax incentives for private long-term care insurance to let Older Americans keep more of what they have earned over the years.

8. The Job Creation and Wage Enhancement Act

Small business incentives, capital gains cut and indexation, neutral cost recovery, risk assessment/cost-benefit analysis, strengthening the Regulatory Flexibility Act and unfunded mandate reform to create jobs and raise worker wages.

9. The Common Sense Legal Reform Act

"Loser pays" laws, reasonable limits on punitive damages and reform of product liability laws to stem the endless tide of litigation.

10. The Citizen Legislature Act

A first-ever vote on term limits to replace career politicians with citizen legislators.

Further, we will instruct the House Budget Committee to report to the floor and we will work to enact additional budget savings, beyond the budget cuts specifically included in the legislation described above, to ensure that the Federal budget deficit will be less than it would have been without the enactment of these bills.

Respecting the judgment of our fellow citizens as we seek their mandate for reform, we hereby pledge our names to this Contract with America.

When the first workers were hired, our entrepreneur would have to place a help-wanted ad that satisfied the nondiscrimination standards of the Equal Employment Opportunity Commission. Her workplace would have to meet local fire safety standards and might come under the regulatory purview of the federal Occupational Safety and Health Administration. If the manufacturing process produced emissions or waste products, local environmental permits would be required; if potential pollution was likely to cross state lines, federal permits might be required as well.

But if the business failed, the owner and the employees would be protected and aided by a number of government programs. The owner could file for bankruptcy protection to preserve personal assets from creditors and perhaps to allow the business to reorganize and get up and running again. The contributions that had been made to worker pensions would probably be protected by ERISA, a federal program created by the Employee Retirement Income Security Act of 1974. Social Security would be available for eligible employees in retirement whether or not they had an adequate pension from the company. Employees thrown out of work when the company failed would be entitled to unemployment compensation for a period of time specified by Congress. State and federal programs would help them locate new jobs and, if necessary, train to acquire new skills.

A hundred years ago, Americans enjoyed much broader economic freedom than they do now. The workplace and the marketplace were less constrained by laws and regulations. However, there was far more risk and danger then than now. Business failure often left owners bankrupt and employees with no sources of income or sustenance. Employees had few rights and often worked long hours at high risk. Employers could and did discriminate in their hiring practices, against women, blacks, the Irish, Jews, and others. Consumers enjoyed few safeguards. Advertising was often untruthful, products frequently failed to live up to their promises and some were downright dangerous. Prices, too, were often artificially high because of monopolistic business practices. The so-called free market was freer for large corporate monopolies than for their competitors or their customers.

Today government is the central and most powerful actor in the American economy. It is the largest employer, the largest spender, the largest lender, and the largest debtor. Few aspects of economic activity are beyond the scope of government regulation. Most Americans pay a significant portion of their annual incomes in taxes; most receive thousands of dollars worth of government benefits. Pure economic freedom has diminished over the twentieth century; but security, stability, protection, and economic opportunity have expanded.

Unlike countries whose twentieth-century economies were shaped by some dominant economic theory—socialism, communism, or fascism, for example—American economic development has been more practical and adaptive. Though American political leaders latched on to theoretical justifications when it served their purposes, the burgeoning of government's role in the economy was accomplished piecemeal over time. America had no Marx; it had no labor party.

What America had was a twentieth-century political system that was remarkably responsive to the demands of particularistic interests. It responded to those interests with individual programs to serve them: antitrust laws to aid the victims of monopolies; new rights for workers and their unions, public-sector jobs for victims of the depression, housing and education subsidies for veterans, regulations to protect consumers and the environment, prohibitions on discrimination against women and minorities. It was politics more than economic theory that changed the relationship between government and the economy in twentieth-century America. It took a century of political debate, not a revolution, to get from 1890 to 1990.

The debate proceeded and the government role in the economy steadily expanded because, to most Americans, it worked. Americans love to complain about big government and heavy taxes. The reality, however, is that Americans have enjoyed enormous increases in their standard of living and personal income during the twentieth century. From 1929 through 1992, for example, disposable personal income, controlled for inflation, increased almost threefold. All of this has occurred with a tax burden that is one of the lightest among the industrialized democracies.

But there are costs as well as benefits in this history. If Americans as a whole are wealthier than they have ever been, that wealth is not evenly distributed among them. A small portion of the American people control a large portion of the country's wealth. In 1991, the top 20 percent of all families received 44.2 percent of all the money income; the lowest fifth received only 4.5 percent— that is, the top fifth of the population earned almost ten times as much as the bottom fifth. Five percent of the population had family incomes of at least $103,000; 12 percent had incomes lower than the federal poverty level of $12,812. Some Americans enjoy lives of opulence; others, however, lack even the basics of a good life.

The pattern of American economic development has broader costs as well. Because economic changes have been stimulated primarily by responses to interest-group demands—by politics rather than economic or political philosophy— the character of economic policy is powerfully shaped by the contemporary political process and by the current alignment of political forces. And in recent decades, American politicians have struggled more than ever before to generate consensus and leadership. The disarray of contemporary political parties, the weakening of executive and legislative leadership institutions, and the growing strength of special-interest groups have had a profound effect on American economic policymaking. They have strengthened the hands of those who sought more economic benefits from the government—more subsidies, more regulations, more protections in the workplace or the marketplace—while weakening the hands of those who sought responsibly to pay the bills for all those programs.

The American people have simultaneously asked the government for more benefits and lower taxes. And government, in the absence of a potent and responsible center, has granted both demands. The consequence of that has been a growing gap between what government costs and what citizens pay. We measure this most commonly in swelling annual budget deficits and accumulating federal debts.

Conclusion

In this chapter we have reviewed a century of the changing relationship between government and the economy. The outcome has been a kind of mixed economy, perhaps we might better call it a political economy. Most of the means of production continue to be privately owned. Participants in the economy, businesses and consumers especially, have a good deal of freedom in the choices they make. But the government is somehow always present, shaping if not controlling the millions of decisions and transactions that occur every day. In the next chapter, we examine the principal ways in which the federal government makes economic policy, how it performs the functions and responsibilities it has acquired over a century of growth and change.

3

....

Making Economic Policy

But while they prate of economic laws, men and
women are starving. We must lay hold of the fact that
economic laws are not made by nature. They are made
by human beings.

—Franklin D. Roosevelt

A LITTLE AFTER 10 P.M. on August 5, 1993, Marjorie Margolies-Mezvinsky, a freshman Democrat, walked into the well of the House of Representatives. She was surrounded by dozens of fellow members shouting at her, pleading with her to vote their way. It had come to this. The new president of the United States had proposed a comprehensive economic program. His party held majorities in both houses of Congress. But after months of debate, negotiation, and revision, the proposal was one vote short of a certain majority. Margolies-Mezvinsky would determine whether the nation was to pursue the economic program of its president—or not.

Despite great pressure from her constituents and many of her colleagues to vote against it—as forty-one other Democrats did—Margolies-Mezvinsky voted for the president's plan. By this hair's breadth, the government adopted a plan to reduce the federal budget deficit by $496 billion over five years, to raise income taxes on the wealthy and other taxes on all Americans, and to cut spending on Medicare and other federal programs. Had Margolies-Mezvinsky voted no, the efforts of the president to lead in economic policymaking—despite public expectation that he should do so, despite majorities of his own party in Congress—would have failed.

The central fact of economic policymaking in the federal government is this: No one dominates. Nowhere is the separation of powers, the competition for power, more evident than in the struggle to determine the shape of American economic policies. Everyone fights. And they fight with all the resources—and resourcefulness—they can bring to bear on these critical decisions that significantly affect the total amount and distribution of wealth in America and the world.

The press often speaks of the "president's economic policy." And it is certainly true that the economic policies of any era usually carry the label of the incumbent president. But presidents must compete for control of economic policy with an array of formidable opponents both inside and outside of government. Congress is full of members—some of them well positioned, terrifically crafty, and very powerful—who have their own views about economic policy. Members of a president's administration often disagree about the

75

proper course of economic policy, and those disagreements may affect their support and enthusiasm even after decisions seem to have been made. State and local governments, business corporations, and special-interest groups also participate aggressively in economic policy struggles. And then there are individual American citizens whose daily lives are affected by the taxes they owe, the interest rates they earn on their savings and pay to borrow money, the pace at which the price of goods and services inflates, and the general health of the economy in which they work.

Struggles over economic policy are a constant of American politics, and they are fought on several important battlefields. One is **fiscal policy,** the annual decisions about federal spending and federal revenues. Another is **monetary policy,** which includes decisions about the supply of money available to the economy and the rates charged to borrowers for its use. A third is **microeconomic policy,** decisions by the government that directly affect particular elements of the economy: regulation, subsidies, bailouts, or focused loan programs, for example.

In this chapter we look at policymaking in each of these areas—fiscal, monetary, and microeconomic policy—and at the peculiar alignment of forces that affects decisionmaking in each.

Fiscal Policy

The principal instrument of U.S. fiscal policy is the federal budget. The budget is a collection of presidential initiatives, congressional actions, and economic conditions. Despite recent efforts to centralize and rationalize budgeting, the budget is still the product of more than a dozen separate pieces of legislation, an even larger number of spending decisions by executive agencies, and thousands of private economic choices. Because these are intensely political decisions, the federal budget is the sum of hundreds of political negotiations and compromises.

The federal government budgets for one fiscal year at a time. The **fiscal year** (FY) starts on the first of October and ends on the last day of September. Each fiscal year takes the number of the calendar year in which it ends; so, for example, fiscal year 1996 begins on October 1, 1995, and ends on September 30, 1996.

For fiscal policy purposes, the budget has three principal elements. The first is spending. The level and purposes of federal spending are formally determined in legislation called **appropriations.** The Constitution is quite clear on this. Article 1, Section 9, says: "No money shall be drawn from the Treasury, but in consequence of appropriations made by law." Normally, no agency of the government may spend federal funds until a law has been passed granting it authority to do so.

In budget terminology, spending decisions are expressed in two ways. One is **budget authority.** These are the sums that agencies are authorized to spend sometime after the appropriation has become law, but not necessarily in the next fiscal year. Some federal projects take more than one year to complete. The construction of an aircraft carrier, for example, might take five years. Those who drafted the defense appropriation act would include budget authority for the full anticipated cost of the aircraft carrier, knowing that the money would be spent over a period of several years. Monies designated for expenditure in a particular fiscal year are called **outlays.** If an aircraft carrier costs $5 billion and takes five years to construct and $1 billion of that amount is to be paid out to the shipyard building the carrier in fiscal year 1996, the appropriation act will include budget authority of $5 billion and an outlay for FY 1996 of $1 billion. The amount of money the federal government spends in FY 1996 is a combination of outlays appropriated in all the FY 1996 appropriation acts plus outlays left over from budget authority created in appropriation acts for previous years. Figure 3.1 shows how this affects all federal spending.

The second major element of the budget is **receipts** (revenues). Receipts are the money the government collects from all sources to fund its operations. Primary among these are the revenues identified in Figure 3.2, which come from the following sources:

- Individual income taxes: the amounts paid to the federal government by individuals' taxes though withholding from their paychecks and filing of annual income tax returns.
- Corporate income taxes: the amounts paid by business corporations based on their profits and operating deductions.
- **Payroll taxes** (social insurance receipts): money withheld from paychecks for specific federal programs such as Social Security or Medicare.
- **Excise taxes:** amounts paid at the time of purchase of goods such as tobacco, gasoline, liquor, and certain luxury items.
- Customs duties: amounts paid by importers as a fee for bringing goods into the United States.
- Borrowing: the monies the federal government borrows to cover the deficit or gap between spending and all other revenues. (Note that in determining annual budget deficits or surpluses, borrowing is not included

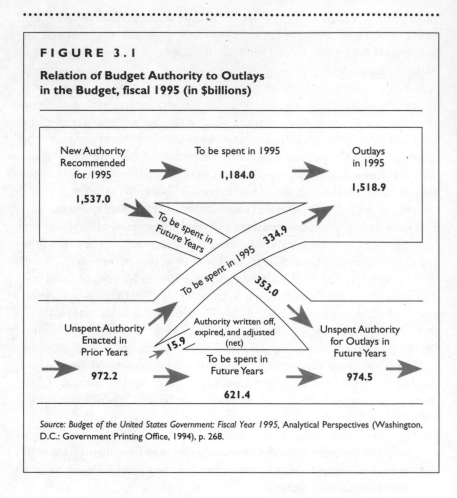

FIGURE 3.1

**Relation of Budget Authority to Outlays
in the Budget, fiscal 1995 (in $billions)**

New Authority
Recommended
for 1995

1,537.0

To be spent in 1995

1,184.0

Outlays
in 1995

1,518.9

To be spent in
Future Years

To be spent in 1995   334.9

353.0

Unspent Authority
Enacted in
Prior Years

972.2

Authority written off,
expired, and adjusted
(net)

15.9

To be spent in
Future Years

621.4

Unspent Authority
for Outlays in
Future Years

974.5

Source: *Budget of the United States Government: Fiscal Year 1995,* Analytical Perspectives (Washington,
D.C.: Government Printing Office, 1994), p. 268.

as a source of revenue. It is the difference between what the government
takes in and what it spends in years in which spending exceeds revenues.)

Federal revenue policies are enacted by law and then remain in effect until
subsequently amended. They need not be reenacted every year. In practice,
however, the government does alter its revenue policies almost every year.
These alterations tend not to change the basic revenue sources but to modify
certain provisions of the revenue laws in order to encourage some kinds of economic activity and discourage others. These usually take the form of minor
tinkering, as in 1992 when President George Bush initiated a reduction in in-

FIGURE 3.2

Sources of Federal Government Revenue, Fiscal 1995

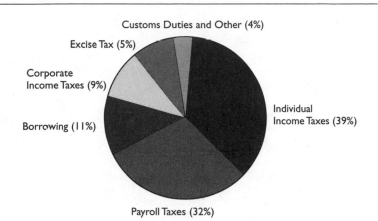

Customs Duties and Other (4%)

Excise Tax (5%)

Corporate
Income Taxes (9%)

Borrowing (11%)

Individual
Income Taxes (39%)

Payroll Taxes (32%)

Source: Adapted from *Budget of the United States Government: Fiscal Year 1995* (Washington, D.C.: Government Printing Office, 1994), p. 12.

come tax–withholding requirements to put more money immediately into the hands of individual citizens. Sometimes they involve a major revision of revenue policies, as in 1986, when a comprehensive tax reform included sweeping provisions to reduce tax rates and limit deductions.

The frequency of adjustment of personal income tax policies is suggested in Figure 3.3, which shows changes in the highest marginal tax rates since the income tax was established in 1913.

The interplay of the first two elements of the budget, outlays and receipts, produces the third: the surplus or deficit, which is the difference between them. The government frequently experienced budget surpluses in the nineteenth century, when federal expenditures were much smaller than they are today and revenues were drawn almost entirely from customs duties. Even as recently as the years from 1920 through 1930, there was a budget surplus every year. But the last federal budget surplus was in FY 1969. There has been a deficit every year since then, and it is not likely that the federal government will run a

FIGURE 3.3

Changes in Marginal Tax Rates and Highest Tax Brackets, 1913–1993
(marginal tax rate on taxable income of more than . . .)

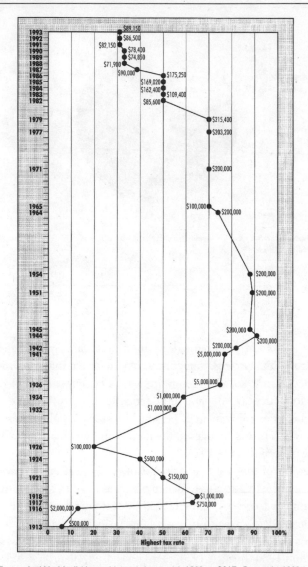

budget surplus again in the foreseeable future. So, for purposes of our discussion here, we will focus primarily on federal deficits.

Now that the activities encompassed in the federal budget are such a large portion of all American economic activity, the size of the deficit can have a significant impact on the health of the American economy. Hence the deficit is an important point of focus for participants in the budget process. As Figure 3.4 demonstrates, deficits in the 1980s and 1990s have been unprecedented for peacetime.

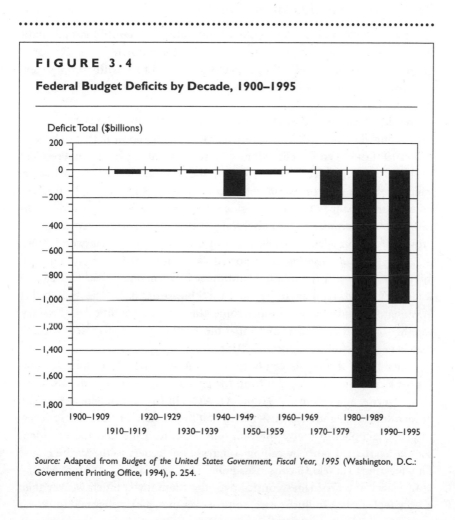

FIGURE 3.4

Federal Budget Deficits by Decade, 1900–1995

Source: Adapted from *Budget of the United States Government, Fiscal Year, 1995* (Washington, D.C.: Government Printing Office, 1994), p. 254.

Keynesians argued that deficits might sometimes be necessary for economic stimulation. As we saw in Chapter 2, the principal question faced by the presidents who first sought to use the budget to affect the national economy was whether there should be a surplus or a deficit. But now and for the foreseeable future, large deficits seem inevitable. The issue for budgetmakers now is not whether to have a deficit but how to manage the size of the deficit. In the modern budget process, the deficit is the 800-pound gorilla. It affects every major budget decision.

The President and Economic Policy

A legacy of FDR and the Keynesian revolution in economics is that many Americans now hold the president responsible for the state of the economy. When the economy is weak, they expect the president to swiftly propose and gain congressional approval for programs that will restore healthy levels of growth.

President Bush learned this lesson the hard way. Although the 1990–1991 recession ended in March 1991, the recovery was initially so weak that in fall and winter 1991 most people believed the country was still in a recession. President Bush at first responded by downplaying the economy's poor performance, which created a perception among voters that he was insensitive to the economic hardships they felt. The president's approval ratings slipped dramatically and by December an overwhelming 71 percent of surveyed voters disapproved of the president's management of economic policy (Harwood, 1991: p. A16). The *Wall Street Journal* reported, "With news of layoffs and business failures mounting by the month, Americans are demanding that their elected leaders try something—anything—to turn things around. . . . The result is that Washington's leaders now consider some kind of action politically necessary, whether or not they are convinced that the methods being proposed will ultimately be successful" (McQueen, 1991: p. A16).

A member of the Republican National Committee noted, "People are looking for a crisp, precise program from the president to get us out of this recession" (Devroy and Dionne, 1991: pp. A1, A11). In November, Senate Majority Leader Robert Dole advised Bush not to wait for his state-of-the-union address to propose a plan to revive the economy. Instead, Dole said the president should "start right now" by calling congressional leaders to the White House for a meeting to develop a consensus policy (Associated Press, 1991: p. A10).

In reality, the president's control over the economy is much weaker than most people realize. In Bush's case, control over monetary policy and thus over short-term interest rates was strictly in the hands of a very independent Federal Reserve that would not succumb to administration pleas or threats to follow a more expansionary policy. A weak recovery exacerbated the problems of recognition lag. And for political reasons Bush decided to wait until January 1992 to propose an economic plan. Because economic policy normally affects the economy with a lag of six to twenty-four months, a stimulative economic policy should have been implemented shortly before or immediately after the recession's July 1990 start. Even if Congress had approved any necessary legislation swiftly, it would have been March or April before a new economic policy could be enacted. In the most optimistic scenario, any new policy wouldn't have begun to affect the economy until fall 1992, more than two years after the recession had started and, in retrospect, almost a year and a half after the recovery had begun.

In his state-of-the-union address, Bush announced a fiscal stimulus package that included a ninety-day freeze on the imposition of new regulations, a reduction in IRS income tax withholding, a $500 per child increase in personal income tax exemptions, a $5,000 income tax credit for individuals buying a house before the end of 1992, a reduction in the tax rates on **capital gains**,[1] a tax credit of $3,750 to allow the poor to purchase health insurance, and repeal of the luxury tax on boats and airplanes, among other measures. Prior to the address, when decisions were being made at the White House, Bush was in control of his plan. But once he announced it, its fate was largely out of his hands. The president sought political leverage by demanding that Congress act on his plan by March 20, 1992. No one believed that likely. In a presidential election year, the Democrats, who controlled Congress, had little interest in adopting a Republican incumbent's proposals or his timetable. Congress did pass a fiscal stimulus plan, but it was very different from the one Bush proposed, and the president killed it with a veto.

Americans expect the president to take the lead in shaping economic policy, and most presidents try to fill that role. But none of our presidents have been economists, and few have had any significant personal experience in business or finance. To lead in making economic policy, therefore, presidents need help. The modern presidency provides that help in many ways.

The executive office of the president includes several statutory agencies that exist principally to assist the president in economic policymaking. Most prominent of these is the Council of Economic Advisers (CEA), created by the Employment Act of 1946. The CEA is composed of three members, usually professional economists, appointed by the president and confirmed by the Senate. The council also employs a staff of professional economists. The council's primary formal responsibility is to prepare the annual *Economic Report of the President,* which is sent to Congress every January. This report is an analysis of national economic conditions and a description of the president's economic program.

In most administrations, the CEA does much more than this. It is a primary source of economic analysis for the president, conducting studies and gathering data that are often critical to presidential decisions in formulating the government's economic programs. The chair of the council is often a major economic adviser to the president, and the chair's economic philosophies sometimes strongly influence or buttress the president's. Charles Schultze and Michael Boskin—both CEA chairs—were important advisers to Presidents Carter and Bush, for example. The council chair usually participates prominently in the administration's highest economic councils and testifies regularly on Capitol Hill in defense of the administration's economic programs.

On budget matters and a wide range of other economic issues as well, presidents rely heavily on the Office of Management and Budget (OMB). First created as the Bureau of the Budget in 1921 and located in the Treasury Department, this unit quickly became the president's primary agent in dealing with departments and agencies in the formulation of their annual budgets. A small, highly professional agency with a reputation for "neutral competence," the Bureau of the Budget served presidents of both parties with equal diligence. In 1970, the mission of the bureau was broadened and its title changed to the Office of Management and Budget (OMB). It became a more politicized agency than it had been, with more political appointees at the top. But its primary responsibility remained unchanged, and OMB continues to work closely with most presidents to formulate an annual budget and to impose spending discipline on the executive branch.

The director of OMB is often a significant participant in presidential policy-making on economic issues. At the beginning of the Reagan presidency, for example, when efforts were under way to make rapid and major changes in economic policy, the person at the center of administration activity was David Stockman, the director of OMB. *New York Times* reporter Hedrick Smith wrote of Stockman's role: "Reagan's agenda was kept on track—and given life—by David Stockman. No single figure, other than Reagan, was more important to Reagan's early success than Stockman, the cocky, zealous, young budget director whose oversized glasses gave him an owlish look. Without Stockman, the supply-side superachiever, Reagan would have been unable to fashion his first budget proposals and make his running start. Reagan had a vision; Stockman had a strategy" (Smith, 1988: p. 351).

In the cabinet, the principal player in economic policymaking is usually the secretary of the Treasury. For most of the twentieth century, Treasury secretaries have been drawn from the top leadership of finance or industry. Presidents Harding, Coolidge, and Hoover relied heavily on Treasury Secretary Andrew Mellon, a famous banker and financier. Eisenhower's first Treasury secretary, George M. Humphrey, was a banker; so too was C. Douglas Dillon, Kennedy's Treasury secretary. Presidents, with but few exceptions, have sought to choose secretaries who inspired the confidence of the business and investment communities. Some Treasury secretaries have been very influential economic advisers, as John Connally was to Richard Nixon and James Baker to Ronald Reagan. But others have not been close to the presidents they served and have had limited influence in economic-policy decisions. One of the roles of a Treasury secretary is to serve as a liaison to economic interests that may not support the president's economic programs. It is hard for some Treasury secretaries to bridge the gap between ambassador to the opposition and powerful inside adviser to the president. Presidential unhappiness with Treasury secretaries is a recurring phenomenon. Richard Nixon was never satisfied with his first Treasury secretary, Roger Kennedy, and eased him into an ambassadorship in the third year of the administration. President Carter fired his first Treasury secretary, Michael Blumenthal.

Other department and agency heads also participate in economic policymaking, their roles shifting depending on the issue and the personal relationship between the president and the individual appointee. In the Clinton administration, for example, Secretary of Labor Robert Reich has been an important economic adviser—far more important than most labor secretaries in other administrations. This resulted in no small part from Reich's prominence as a scholar and writer before entering government and from his long personal friendship with President Clinton.

A major problem confronting all presidents is not too little economic advice but too much. Every modern administration is full of bright people anxious to try to persuade the president to undertake the economic policies they favor. The trouble is that they rarely agree on what those policies should be. The director of OMB may be primarily concerned about deficit reduction. The secretary of labor is worried most about job growth. The secretary of the Treasury is most concerned about interest rates. And the chair of the Council of Economic Advisers wants to stimulate long-term growth in productivity. To meet a variety of economic goals, presidents must find ways to coordinate and balance the advice they receive in order to formulate a consensus or compromise that facilitates decisionmaking.

That has been achieved in recent administrations by the creation of coordinating councils at the highest levels of the administration. These are not statutory bodies; they are created by each administration to fit its own particular needs and to include the participants that each president wants involved. President Ford, for example, created an Economic Policy Board for this purpose. President Reagan relied on a cabinet council on economic policy. President Clinton has used an interagency group called the National Economic Council to broker the differing economic views of administration members.

Despite all the advice available to them and their ingenuity in devising mechanisms for receiving and coordinating it, presidents often find that economic decisionmaking is frustrating. Economics is an inexact science. Conflicting objectives can never be fully resolved. The consequences of presidential decisions can never be predicted with total confidence. Ronald Reagan noted when his tax-cut program was initiated in 1981, for example, that his plan would accelerate economic recovery because businesses would get a larger return on their investments and consumers would be able to keep—and to spend or save—more of their earnings. What happened instead was a quaking of the financial markets in the face of steeply rising federal deficits. Reagan was forced to return to Congress within a year with a $16 billion deficit-reduction package.

Presidents must often choose a course of action knowing that its consequences or side effects may come back to haunt later on. Richard Nixon imposed a program of wage and price controls in 1971. It slowed inflation for a while but also produced pent-up price pressures that reemerged when the controls were lifted. Even the most adroit exercise of leadership may not yield favorable economic conditions because the range of tools available to the government are so limited and the constraints on using them are so large. This is a central dilemma of economic policymaking: Authority does not equal responsibility. The tools of economic leadership are rarely adequate to meet the expectations imposed on economic leaders.

The Budget Process

It takes about eighteen months to construct each federal budget. While one budget is wending its way through Congress, the next is already under development in the executive branch. The budget cycle is one of the inevitable routines of government. It is also the most potent. Nothing else so powerfully affects what the government does. The budget is where real priorities are established. Because of the importance of the annual budget, executive agencies and congressional committees spend much of their time working on it.

To trace the budget process, let's take a hypothetical fiscal year that we'll call FY 2000. FY 2000 begins on October 1, 1999, and ends on September 30, 2000. To do its job properly, the government should enact the federal budget for FY 2000 before that fiscal year begins. So in budgeting for FY 2000, October 1, 1999, is a very important target date.

To get a budget prepared by October 1, 1999, Congress will need to begin its own deliberations in January 1999. But on what does it deliberate? Most of the time its deliberations begin with a document prepared by the Office of Management and Budget and approved by the president, in this case called *The Budget of the United States, Fiscal Year 2000*. This document (which may include several different volumes of varying detail) is actually the president's recommendation to Congress for what the budget should be for FY 2000. Since the Budget and Accounting Act of 1921, presidents have been required to submit an annual budget recommendation to Congress. The deadline for that submission is the first Monday in February.

But the president's budget doesn't just materialize out of nowhere. It is the product of months of work in the executive branch, beginning at the lowest levels in the departments and agencies and working up through the hierarchy until the president and his economic advisers become directly involved. The process thus begins in the executive branch sixteen to eighteen months before the starting date of the new fiscal year.

Summer 1998: Agency Preparation. The formal budget process begins in the summer before the budget is submitted to Congress. In spring, OMB has analyzed the economic conditions projected for the next fiscal year. It has sought to determine the president's economic objectives and opportunities and his programmatic priorities. From these deliberations it develops a budget "mark" for each agency. This is a maximum spending figure it assigns to the agency to guide its own decisions. The agency has some latitude in determining how to allocate its own spending within the mark, but the mark is intended to be the maximum it can spend.

Most agencies think their mark is too low; they want to spend more money than OMB has allotted them at this stage. So much of what follows over the next several months involves efforts by agencies to justify more spending than OMB wants.

Fall 1998: OMB Review of Agency Budgets. Agencies submit their budgets to OMB in September. Each is then carefully reviewed by OMB employees called **budget examiners.** These are typically professional career employees of OMB who work with the same agency every year. Budget examiners acquire broad expertise about the programs and personnel of the agencies they review. They work closely with agency budget officers to bring the budget into line with OMB's expectations. In the weeks that follow these submissions, OMB accepts some agency budgets, rejects others and returns them for more work, and makes alterations in others.

December 1998–January 1999: Final Adjustments. When OMB cuts or otherwise alters agency budget submissions, agencies often fight back by appealing directly to the president or seeking the assistance of some powerful administration figure to plead their case. The final deliberations on the budget in the executive branch occur in the two months before it is submitted to Congress. They result in almost daily adjustments and compromises designed to match what the agencies want with the spending, revenue, and deficit totals upon which the president has decided. It is often a time of intense political infighting in the White House, with the agencies and departments on one side, seeking a larger share of the budget, and OMB on the other, seeking to impose overall budget discipline.

February 1999: Submission of the FY 2000 Budget to Congress. On the first Monday in February the president's FY 2000 budget is presented to Congress and the public with great fanfare. At roughly the same time, two other important events are occurring. One is the publication of the *Economic Report of the President,* which provides the Council of Economic Advisers' forecasts of economic conditions for the coming year. The other is an important preliminary analysis of the new budget and the state of the economy by a congressional agency called the Congressional Budget Office (CBO). Many consider the CBO to be the legislative counterpart to OMB and the CEA. CBO's task is to provide Congress with an objective analysis of the budget and the economy. It was created in 1974 by a Congress that felt that the forecasts and analyses it received from the president's advisory bodies were often biased in support of the president's proposals. Now when Congress begins to consider the budget it has not only the analyses of OMB and the CEA but also of its own budget office, the CBO.

February–May 1999: Congressional Budget Deliberations, Track 1. The budget process in Congress proceeds on two tracks, often simultaneously. In one track, the House and Senate Budget Committees focus on the budget in quite broad terms. Their task is to set overall totals for expenditures, revenues, and the size of the deficit. In this, the committees are sometimes bound by statutes or earlier budget agreements fixing spending levels for certain programs. Within the overall totals they set, the Budget Committees also recommend expenditure ceilings in broad programmatic categories.

The primary focus of the Budget Committees is the preparation of a **concurrent resolution on the budget.** In practice, this serves as the congressional budget, providing guidance in the deliberations that follow on several items: revenues, new budget authority, outlays, the size of the deficit, the national debt, and federal credit activities.

The Budget Committees also allocate the overall totals to each of twenty different functions such as agriculture, national defense, and energy. In addition, the committees provide **reconciliation** instructions. These are directives to individual House or Senate committees to raise revenues or cut spending in specific ways in order to meet the Budget Committee's overall revenue or deficit targets.

The Budget Reform Act of 1974 called for the Budget Committees to report the concurrent resolution on the budget by April 1 so that both houses could vote on it by April 15, but those deadlines are rarely met. Contention over these very important decisions frequently slows the decisionmaking process.

February–October 1999: Congressional Budget Deliberations, Track 2. The second budget track is the scrutiny of individual agency budgets by the subcommittees of the House and Senate Appropriations Committees, and eventually by the full Congress. In theory, the review of agency budgets is supposed to follow the budget resolution and be guided by it. In practice, the Appropriations Committees begin their work before the budget resolution is passed. In the first few months of the congressional session, therefore, budget activity is occurring all over Capitol Hill.

The detail work of the budget process is done by the subcommittees of the House and Senate Appropriations Committees. There are thirteen of these subcommittees in each house and they are among the most important and powerful bodies in Congress. Each subcommittee has jurisdiction over a set of federal programs and agencies. For example, the Energy and Water Development Appropriations Subcommittee has jurisdiction over a wide range of agencies including the Army Corps of Engineers, the Bureau of Reclamation, the Energy Department, and the Tennessee Valley Authority.

Membership on the Appropriations subcommittees is quite stable, and because members are long serving, they develop a good deal of expertise about the programs in their jurisdiction. It is not uncommon for the senior members of an Appropriations subcommittee to know more about an agency and its programs than the appointee who heads it. The hearings held by these subcommittees to review agency budgets often involve a grilling of agency officials who are required to justify their expenditure recommendations. Sometimes the subcommittee members think the agencies are seeking too much money and impose cuts. But sometimes, as well, subcommittee members want larger expenditures for programs they favor and require agency officials to explain why their recommendations are not higher. The latter pattern is especially common when the program under consideration is one that benefits the state or district represented by a member of an Appropriations subcommittee.

Some members, in fact, expend significant energy trying to get funds earmarked for projects in the state or district they represent. An **earmark** is language in an appropriations bill that requires a specified amount of money to be spent in a specified way and place. In 1991, for example, the chair of the House Defense Appropriations Subcommittee, Representative John Murtha (D–Pa.), helped his Pennsylvania colleague, Representative Paul Kanjorski (D–Pa.) secure an earmark providing $20 million to create "an advanced technology demonstration facility for environmental technology." It further specified that "these funds are to be provided only to the organization known as Earth Conservancy in Hanover Township, Pennsylvania" (Weiner, 1994: p. A1).

Because appropriations are rarely enacted without the support of the subcommittees that have jurisdiction over them, the members of those subcommittees have significant influence on the budget process. Especially influential are the chairs of the Appropriations subcommittees. In recent years, the chairs of the House Appropriations subcommittees have sometimes been called the **college of cardinals** because of their prominence in the budget process.

The principal work of the Appropriations Committees is to prepare the thirteen annual appropriations bills through which the Congress legislates expenditures. In theory, these bills are to be "reported out" (sent to the floor for a vote) by the Appropriations Committees and voted upon by the Congress by early summer. That rarely happens, however. Some appropriations bills are not approved until the very end of the legislative session. Others are passed by Congress, then vetoed by the president and sent back for reconsideration. Because these are usually the most important pieces of legislation passed in each session of Congress, debate is contentious, consensus is elusive, and deliberation drags on. Of the thirteen appropriations bills for FY 1994, for example, only two were signed into law before the beginning of the fiscal year.

August–September 1999: Reconciliation. As the appropriations bills begin to emerge, the budget committees undertake their second function. That is to ensure that the totals in the appropriations bills are reconciled with the overall targets for revenues, outlays, and the deficit. This is accomplished through enactment of a reconciliation bill.

The reconciliation bill is often the most important and the most difficult step in the budget process. To bring the individual totals in line with the overall totals, it is usually necessary to increase revenues, cut spending, or enlarge the deficit. None of those options is appealing to most members of Congress, so there is often heavy combat over reconciliation. This chapter began with a description of the narrow margin by which the 1993 reconciliation bill sustained President Bill Clinton's economic program. That battle was illustrative of the difficulty that is normal at this stage of the budget process.

October 1, 1999: Fiscal Year 2000 begins. The new fiscal year begins on October 1, even if all the appropriations bills have not been passed. When Congress has failed to complete action on an appropriations bill before the start of a new fiscal year, the affected agencies have no authority to spend funds. To keep them from simply shutting down, Congress usually passes a stopgap measure called a **continuing resolution.** A continuing resolution provides funding for an agency, usually at the same level as the previous year, until its new appropriation is enacted.

Described in bare outline like this, the budget process seems carefully timed and well organized. In fact, no close observer would describe it that way. It is instead a kind of loosely structured, ongoing political battle. The skirmishes over dollar decisions reflect critically important choices about how public monies will be spent to accomplish policy objectives. Every one of those choices is controversial; nearly all have at least two opposing sides. Budget and appropriations decisions yield winners and losers. So everyone fights to get as much money as they can for the programs they like and to hold the line on or cut the programs they don't.

All of this slows the budget process, sometimes to a standstill. In 1990, for example, the process of deliberation simply broke down. Only an extraordinary budget summit at Andrews Air Force Base and other places away from Capitol Hill permitted administration and congressional leaders to get around a profound budget impasse. It is frustrating to participants that decisionmaking is so difficult and time-consuming. Equally frustrating in recent years has been the failure of the budget process to bring the deficit under control. These frustrations have led to several major efforts to reform the budget process.

Budget Reform

The shape of the current budget process grew out of the first of those reform efforts. In 1974, Congress passed the Congressional Budget Reform and

Impoundment Control Act. This legislation created the Congressional Budget Office to give Congress its own objective source of economic analysis. It established the budget timetable previously described and created new Budget Committees in the House and Senate. And it limited a practice that most presidents had used up to that time of delaying the spending of appropriated funds (**deferrals**) or deciding never to spend money that had been appropriated (**rescissions**). Together, deferrals and rescissions are called **impoundments** of funds. The Budget Reform Act required that most such impoundments be subjected to congressional scrutiny before taking effect.

Deficits continued to grow in the decade after passage of the Budget Reform Act. The disciplines of the reform act were observed only loosely. So in 1985, Congress adopted a new reform approach proposed by Senators Phil Gramm (R–Tex.), Warren Rudman (R–N.H.), and Ernest Hollings (D–S.C.). This was the Balanced Budget and Emergency Deficit Control Act of 1985, but it came to be called the **Gramm-Rudman-Hollings Act (GRH)**. GRH proposed to eliminate the federal deficit in equal amounts of $36 million a year over five years, thus balancing the budget by 1991. The unique provision of GRH was its mandatory deficit-cutting procedure that came into play if Congress failed to meet its deficit-reduction targets. Such failure would trigger a **sequester** of appropriated funds—in effect, a mandatory, across-the-board spending cut. More than forty-five programs, including Social Security, were exempted from the sequester process, but all others were subjected to it.

GRH was enacted quickly and without much deliberation in 1985. By the end of 1986, some of its procedures were declared unconstitutional by the Supreme Court. In constructing the FY 1987 budget, Congress used a number of dodges and artifices to avoid almost $20 billion in mandated across-the-board spending cuts.

Artful dodging continued in the FY 1988 budget. The GRH medicine was simply too strong for Congress; the political costs of meeting the GRH targets were too high. By 1990, GRH was in deep disrepair, a fact clearly demonstrated by the breakdown in that year's budget process.

The 1990 budget crisis led to further tinkering with the budget process. The burgeoning of the federal deficit in 1990 combined with prevailing fears about the potential political impact of a GRH sequester led to several weeks of intense negotiations between Bush administration officials and congressional leaders behind closed doors. What resulted was an agreement to cut spending, including spending on some entitlement programs, and to raise revenues.

More important, Congress sought to prevent such crises in the future by adding Title 13 to the 1990 Omnibus Budget Reconciliation Act (OBRA). This was the most significant alteration of the budget process since 1974. It placed caps on **discretionary spending** (spending not mandated by existing laws) for the years 1991–1995. It also established a **pay-as-you-go** principal requiring that bills providing increases in discretionary spending or decreases in revenues be accompanied by offsetting adjustments elsewhere in the same program category or they could be ruled out of order. And it granted broader powers to the president to enforce the disciplines it sought to establish.

Some political leaders have suggested that tinkering with budget procedures is not going to change the fundamental incentives under which presidents and members of Congress operate. This is a major dilemma of economic policy-making. Whatever the process, the fact remains that it is easier politically to vote for spending increases than spending cuts, for tax cuts than tax increases. Those incentives make it very hard for politicians to discipline themselves to bring the budget back into balance after several decades of deficit financing. To some, that has suggested the need for stronger medicine: an amendment to the Constitution mandating a balanced budget.

dilemma

"EVERYBODY WANTS TO GO TO HEAVEN, BUT NOBODY WANTS TO DIE."

In the last two decades of the twentieth century, there has been broad support for the need to balance the budget but little consensus on the best way to accomplish that. Reprinted by permission of the *Los Angeles Times,* Los Angeles Times Syndicate.

Several times in the 1980s and 1990s, the Congress considered a **balanced-budget amendment** to the Constitution that would require the government to keep revenues and expenditures in balance except in times of emergency. Because many voters see the balanced-budget amendment as the only effective cure for the government's constant deficit spending, it has much political appeal. When the proposal was last seriously considered in 1995, it received overwhelming support in the House of Representatives but fell just short in the Senate of the two-thirds majority necessary to amend the Constitution. At the time, the only way to close a deficit of more than $190 billion would have been draconian cuts in spending or major tax increases. When the debate on the balanced-budget amendment came to a showdown, some interest groups that feared significant loss of federal benefits—the elderly, for example—lobbied aggressively against passage.

Budgeting aggravates and illumines all the stress points of government. Deliberations on the federal budget differ from virtually all other forms of government decisionmaking because they are action-forcing. We have to have a budget or we don't have a government. When conflict arises on other matters, it can be dealt with by delay or avoidance: Don't act now or don't act at all. For decades, for example, conflict over national health insurance was contained by inaction.

The budget permits no such easy out. The federal government raises and spends more than a $1.5 trillion each year. All of its citizens have a direct and often compelling interest in who pays how much and who gets how much. It is not surprising that conflict is so common and consensus so rare.

The budget process evolves regularly because we keep trying to find structural and procedural ways to channel and resolve budget conflict. Procedural innovations often fail because we are as ingenious in dodging their disciplines as we are in inventing them. The budget process described here differs from the one we would have described a decade ago, and it probably differs as well from the one that will be in place a decade after you read this. What endures—the constants of budgeting—are not the procedural details but the political realities. Government wants more of our wealth in taxes than we want to pay; it is willing to spend less on programs we favor than we think they deserve. So conflict will continue to course through the budget process. And government leaders will continue to seek new ways to produce the budgets that conflict makes so difficult to create.

Tax Policy

Tax policymaking is not governed by the same routines as the budget process. Nor is there a comprehensive review of tax policies every year as there is of expenditures. Tax policymaking is episodic. Some alterations in tax policy occur almost every year; major alterations occur less frequently.

Most proposals for changes in revenue policy initiate with the president. In weighing revenue proposals, presidents typically rely on the economic advisers identified earlier in this chapter. Tax policy is, after all, an important component of government economic policy. When focusing on tax policy, presidents are also likely to seek advice from the assistant secretary of the Treasury for tax policy and the commissioner of internal revenue, who heads the federal government's tax-collection agency, the Internal Revenue Service (IRS).

Some changes in tax policy are primarily technical. They are designed to make revenue collection more efficient, to close loopholes that unintentionally allow some people to avoid taxes, or to clarify existing regulations. Other changes, usually the most significant, are undertaken to affect the private economy. Tax policy is sometimes used as an instrument of fiscal policy. Taxes may be reduced or collected more slowly to stimulate private economic activity. Taxes may be raised or collected more rapidly to slow the economy or to permit a higher level of expenditure or accomplish a smaller deficit.

The president's proposals for changes in tax policy go to Congress, where they come under the jurisdiction of two very powerful committees. The Constitution specifies in Article 1, Section 7, that "all bills for raising revenue shall originate in the House of Representatives; but the Senate may propose or concur with amendments as on other bills." Action begins, therefore, with the Ways and Means Committee in the House.

Ways and Means is a large committee and its membership usually has a larger proportion of members from the majority party than does the House as a whole. In 1995, for example, Republicans composed 53 percent of all House members, but 59 percent of the thirty-six members of Ways and Means. By tradition, members of Ways and Means tend to be more senior, more independent, and more conservative than most of their colleagues. The committee guards its power and prerogatives jealously and is rarely reluctant to oppose or alter presidential tax initiatives. In his 1992 state-of-the-union address, for example, President Bush proposed a set of economic-growth measures that included seven changes in tax policy. These proposals went first to the Ways and Means Committee, where they were quickly replaced by a different set of initiatives favored by the Democratic majority on the committee. The bill that finally emerged from Congress was so different from his original proposals that President Bush vetoed it.

The Senate Finance Committee is a potent force as well in tax policymaking. Like its House counterpart, its members usually include some of the most senior and economically conservative senators. It, too, takes its role and authority seriously and feels no reluctance to question or oppose presidential proposals.

The House Ways and Means and Senate Finance Committees have enormous jurisdictions and thus profound influence. Each is responsible for all revenue policies. Each is responsible as well for most health care programs like Medicare and Medicaid and for Social Security. Each also has responsibility for most Treasury programs, including debt financing, and each oversees the federal debt. In budget terms, therefore, these two committees have jurisdiction over virtually all revenues, more than half of all expenditures, and the entire federal debt.

When alterations are made in tax policy, they usually involve changes in one of the three principal elements of the income tax structure: (1) **marginal rates,** (2) **tax brackets,** and (3) **exemptions** and **deductions.** The taxes that individuals or corporations pay are determined by a combination of these three elements. What you owe, for example, depends on the bracket in which your income places you, the marginal tax rate for that bracket, and the aspects of your income that are exempt from taxes.

Let us say, to flesh out this example, that in 1993 your income was $80,000, that you were married and filed jointly with your spouse, that you had two children who were your dependents, that you owned a home on which you paid a mortgage, and that you contributed $5,000 to the college you and your spouse had attended. For purposes of this example, we will assume there are no other financial facts about you that affect your taxes. Under the tax policies in effect for 1993, your taxes would have been determined in the way shown in Box 3.1.

Note in this example that most of the $10,351 owed by this family in taxes would have been withheld from the paychecks of the income earners. It often happens, in fact, that more money is withheld than is actually owed. In such cases, taxpayers qualify for a tax refund when they file their tax returns. A refund is the difference between what was withheld from pay checks and what is actually owed.

Also note that this family's average tax rate on its gross income of $80,000 is 13 percent even though its income is technically in a bracket where the marginal tax rate is 28 percent. That is because deductions and exemptions reduce its taxable income from $80,000 to $54,100 and because for 1993 the marginal rate of 28 percent only applied to taxable income above $36,900. Taxable income below $36,900 was taxed at the lower marginal rate of 15 percent.

Marginal tax rates have been adjusted many times since 1913, as indicated in Figure 3.3 earlier in this chapter. Applicable tax brackets have often been

BOX 3.1

Example for Figuring Taxes Owed

Gross income	$80,000
Deductions and exemptions:	
Exemptions for 4 dependents (each worth $2,350)	9,400
Deduction for interest payments on home mortgage	11,500
Deduction for gift to college	5,000
TOTAL deductions and exemptions	25,900
Taxable income (gross income less deductions and exemptions)	54,100
Taxes owed:	
Marginal rate for first tax bracket (up to $36,900) is 15%	5,535
Marginal rate for second tax bracket (remaining $17,200)	
is 28%	4,816
TOTAL tax owed	$10,351

changed as well. Much of the ongoing debate over tax policy involves exemptions and deductions. Some people refer to these exemptions as **tax expenditures.** They argue that there is no practical difference between spending federal funds for some purpose and not collecting taxes on money used for the same purpose. If, for example, the federal government decides to encourage home ownership, it can appropriate funds to subsidize the purchase of homes by individuals or it can exempt from taxes some of what individuals pay for their homes. In fact, this is precisely what the federal government has done, as in our previous example. Federal tax policy allows individuals who itemize deductions on their tax return to exempt from federal income taxes the interest they pay on their mortgage loans. The financial impact on government and on individuals is little different than it would be if the federal government paid a direct subsidy to individuals equal to the amount by which their taxes are reduced. Hence the term "tax expenditures."

There are now many exemptions written into the tax code. Table 3.1 indicates the largest of those in terms of uncollected revenues. Note that the total value of all these tax expenditures in 1994 was $396 billion (U.S. Department

TABLE 3.1

Largest Tax Expenditures and Estimated Revenue Losses in 1994

Item	Revenue Lost (in billions)
Nontaxation of pension contributions and earnings	57.8
Deductibility of mortgage interest on owner-occupied homes	51.8
Exclusion of employer contributions for medical insurance and medical care	51.4
Step-up basis of capital gains at death	26.9
Deductibility of state and local taxes	24.3
Accelerated depreciation of machines and equipment	22.8
Deductibility of charitable contributions	17.3
Nontaxation of Social Security benefits	16.7
Deferral of capital gains on home sales	13.9
Deductibility of property tax on owner-occupied homes	13.9
Deductibility of interest on state and local debt	11.9
Exclusion of interest on life insurance savings	8.1

Source: U.S. Department of Commerce, Bureau of the Census, *Statistical Abstract of the United States, 1994* (Washington, D.C.:Government Printing Office, 1994), p. 336.

of Commerce, 1994: p. 336). This amount significantly exceeds the budget deficit for 1994 of $203 billion.

Tax expenditures exist because they have important political proponents who fight to get them and then to keep them. Some of them, like the mortgage-interest deduction, are very popular and thus difficult to challenge politically. Proponents of tax expenditures argue that they are an efficient way for the federal government to encourage certain kinds of economic activity by lowering its cost to individuals. Because these activities reduce tax liability and thus cost less, individuals are more likely to purchase houses, contribute to charitable and nonprofit organizations, and invest in municipal bonds. If there were no tax exemptions, they argue, fewer homes would get built, many colleges would close, symphonies would fall silent, museums and theaters would go dark, and state and local governments would have trouble undertaking major construction projects.

Critics argue that tax expenditures are often driven by politics more than economic rationality, that they deny large sums of revenue to the federal government and thus contribute significantly to the deficit and the debt, that they are not subject to annual review like regular expenditures that require appropriations, and that they unfairly favor the wealthy. For example, under current tax law, individuals do not have to pay taxes on the interest they pay on a home mortgage, even a mortgage for a vacation home at the seashore. The larger their mortgage, the larger the interest they pay, and the larger their deduction.

But there is no similar exemption for the rent paid by people who live in apartments and do not own their own homes. Since homes, and especially vacation homes, are disproportionately owned by wealthy Americans and renters are disproportionately poorer Americans, tax-expenditure policy in this case is far more valuable to the rich than to the poor. This is a pattern that holds for most tax expenditures: They favor the wealthy over the poor. One recent study determined, for example, that the average value of the mortgage-interest deduction for taxpayers with incomes over $100,000 was $3,469; for taxpayers in the $20,000–$30,000 bracket who qualified to take this deduction, it was worth an average of only $516 (Howe and Longman, 1992: p. 93).

Because tax-policy decisions have such a direct and visible effect on special interests, they are among the most intensely contested of all policy decisions. Even an apparently minor adjustment in tax policy can have an impact that is worth millions of dollars to a corporation or other economic interest. A major tax-reform effort rivets and energizes the political system. Listen to the principal chroniclers of the Tax Reform Act of 1986:

> Even when it came to the hundreds of loopholes benefiting only the narrower and wealthier interests, the politics were difficult. Many Americans resent these special tax breaks, but their elimination is not a top priority for them. The intensity of the beneficiaries of such favors, however, is overwhelming. They marshal sophisticated economic arguments on the economic cataclysms that would result in changing the tax code; some of these claims are even legitimate. If those arguments fail, many of these interests are able to muster something even more persuasive to certain lawmakers: money in the form of campaign contributions.
>
> ... Nowhere are vested interests, through their political action committees, more omnipresent than in tax writing. The possibility of a sweeping tax bill that would touch virtually all these interests brought the campaign money merchants out in droves. In 1985, when the tax-writing panels were considering tax reform, political action committees gave $6.7 million to fifty-six members of the House Ways and Means and Senate Finance committees, according to a reliable survey by the self-styled citizens lobby Common Cause. This was two and a half times more money than was given to members of the same committees two years earlier. Where did the money come from? Insurance companies, banks, oil-and-gas interests, real estate, big Wall Street investment concerns, and labor unions, to name a few—all the groups that would be affected by the tax-reform initiative. (Birnbaum and Murray, 1987: pp. xii–xiii)

There are several characteristics and consequences of these policy struggles that help to define tax policy in the United States. One is that whereas presidents often are the initiators of tax-policy changes, they rarely dominate. Often their initiatives fail to yield the changes they seek. Even when change occurs, it may not be what the president sought. Presidents are influential actors in tax policymaking, but so are the tax committees of Congress. And their interactions are heavily affected by election and interest-group politics.

A second characteristic that emerges from this mix is tax policies that lack economic consistency and rationality. Revenues now regularly fall short of expenditures not because political leaders decided that such a shortfall was prudent for fiscal policy reasons but because the politics of expenditures and the politics of revenues are still separate and distinctive spheres despite recent efforts to bring them closer together. Some forms of income are exempt from taxes and others are not; politics, not economics, usually explains the distinction. Revenue policies shift episodically and usually the changes take effect almost immediately. This complicates corporate and individual efforts to plan investment and savings strategies. Often, in fact, tax policies for a calendar year are not finally determined until the very end of the year, just as the congressional session is ending.

A third characteristic of tax policies is that because of the traditional American resistance to taxes and the political openness of the tax-policy process, tax rates in the United States are lower than in most other industrialized countries. As Figure 3.5 demonstrates, Americans pay a lower percentage of their GDP in taxes than citizens of other developed countries.

Monetary Policy

The Constitution grants to Congress the power to coin money and regulate the value thereof. At first glance, this seems a rather minor and practical responsibility. Over the full course of American history, however, the power to create money—and the way that power has been exercised—have been matters of hot political debate. The existence and survival of the national bank was a dominant political issue during the early decades of the nineteenth century. Later in that century, agrarian interests frequently felt strapped for cash and saw themselves as the victims of the credit policies of eastern financiers. They sought government help in the form of an increased money supply in order to halt deflation. Their favorite approach for expanding the money supply was to end the sole reliance on the gold standard, where all currency had to be backed by reserves of gold, and to permit "free silver" (the unlimited coinage of silver). The

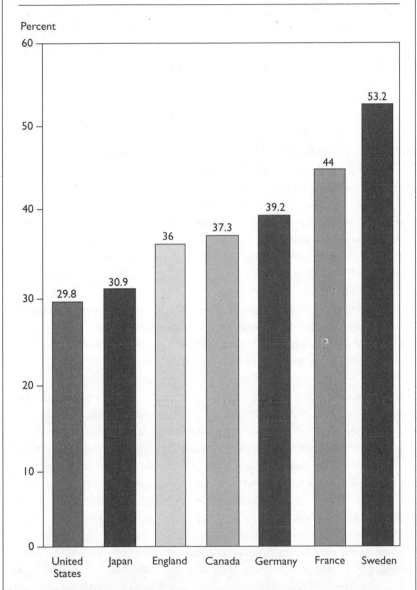

FIGURE 3.5

Tax Revenues as a Percentage of Gross Domestic Product, 1991

Percent

Source: Statistical Abstract of the United States, 1994 (Washington, D.C.: Government Printing Office, 1994), p. 867.

leading spokesman of these approaches was William Jennings Bryan, whose passionate attack on federal monetary policies at the Democratic National Convention in 1896 became known as the "Cross of Gold" speech and catapulted Bryan to national prominence.

In response to erratic changes in the money supply and major recessions caused by a nationwide epidemic of bank failures, particularly the bank panic of 1907, Congress decided in 1913 to delegate authority over monetary policy to the Federal Reserve System.

The Federal Reserve System

At the pinnacle of the Federal Reserve System is the Federal Reserve Board, or "Fed" as it is often called, which is unique among government agencies in structure and authority. The seven members of its Board of Governors are appointed by the president with the advice and consent of the Senate, but the Fed is not part of the executive branch and the president has no statutory authority over its actions beyond his appointment power. Even the appointment power gives the president little control over Fed actions. The individual governors serve single, fourteen-year terms, so presidents have only rare opportunities to change the composition of the board.

The chair of the Federal Reserve Board is appointed by the president to a four-year term, again with the advice and consent of the Senate. But the term of the chair does not align with the president's, so a new president has to wait several years before appointing a new Fed chair.

The Fed is not part of Congress either, though it operates on a direct delegation of Congress's constitutional power to coin money and regulate the value thereof. In fact, Congress has little direct control over the actions of the Fed. It can deny confirmation to presidential appointees, but it does not control the operational budget of the agency. The only real leverage Congress has is its ability to amend the Federal Reserve Act and restructure the Fed to limit its independence. But this is a weak lever, and as a practical matter, the Fed is largely independent of both the president and Congress in its operations.

The Federal Reserve system is an organization of several parts. At the center in Washington is the Board of Governors. The board oversees the operations of the rest of the system. Then there are twelve Federal Reserve banks located around the country that conduct the day-to-day operations of the system. The Board of Governors in Washington supervises many of the operations of the twelve Federal Reserve banks, appoints the chair and vice chair of each bank's own board of directors, and approves all the other major appointments. The system also includes member banks—all the state and nationally chartered banks in the United States.

Some of the most important work of the Fed is conducted by its Federal Open Market Committee (FOMC). The voting membership of this committee is composed of the seven Federal Reserve governors, the president of the Federal Reserve Bank of New York, and four other Federal Reserve bank presidents who serve rotating one-year terms.

The Fed and Monetary Policy

The Fed functions as the central bank of the United States. As such, it is the most influential component of national monetary policy development. The Fed has three principal ways of affecting the supply and availability of money in the national economy. Before we discuss these, we need to explain what we mean by money.

Money is not just coins and bills, though these are certainly one form of money. The Fed measures the quantity of money in the economy in many different ways. A narrow measure is called **M1** and includes paper currency, coins, travelers' checks, and all deposits in checking-type accounts. M1 on any given date is the total of all of these components. A broader measure of the money supply is **M2**, which includes everything in M1 plus funds in small savings accounts, small certificates of deposit (CDs), and money market mutual funds or money market deposit accounts.

The first and most important of the ways in which the Fed influences the money supply is through **open-market operations** conducted under a policy directive issued by the FOMC. The New York Federal Reserve Bank has responsibility for conducting open-market operations. The Fed "creates" money by purchasing Treasury securities in the government securities market. The securities dealers from whom the Fed makes its purchases deposit the payments they receive from the Fed into their own bank accounts. These payments by the Fed create an initial amount of new money in the form of checking deposits that are part of M1. The Fed obtains money to make the payment by simply creating it on computer bookkeeping accounts. Like Rumplestiltskin, spinning straw into gold, the Fed "spins" thin air into newly created bank deposits.[2]

A large fraction of the new deposits created this way can then be lent to borrowers. Through the process of lending deposits initially created by the Fed, additional new deposits are created and in turn lent, resulting in a multiple expansion of the money supply.[3] Borrowers can use the loans to build houses, start new companies, or make any number of purchases that generate economic activity.

Why would the Fed want to increase the money supply? The answer is not always simple, but most of the time it does so to provide a supply of credit adequate to meet the needs of a growing economy while simultaneously maintaining price stability. Sometimes, the Fed may increase the money supply to lower interest rates and stimulate economic activity. Money is a commodity and the cost of borrowing it is measured by the interest rates charged to borrowers. Like other commodities, its cost depends on supply and demand. If the demand for money remains steady, an increase in the money supply should lead to lower interest rates. That is, when more money is available, it should cost less to borrow it. When money costs less, more people will borrow and more funds will be available for investment.

When the Fed sells previously issued Treasury securities to the dealers, they pay the Fed out of their checking accounts and the size of the money stock is initially reduced by the amount of these payments. Because a lower level of deposits limits the lending activity of banks, a multiple contraction of the money supply usually results from this process. The Fed normally seeks to reduce the growth rate in the money supply in order to raise interest rates and limit growth in aggregate demand—usually to prevent undesirable inflation. In 1987–1988, for example, the Fed pursued a more contractionary monetary policy, reducing the growth rates of M1 and M2 by nearly two-thirds of their 1986 values. Most interest rates rose steadily over this time period.

The impacts of changing money-supply growth rates are not always consistent or fully predictable. And the short-run impacts may differ from the long-run impacts. This makes the conduct of discretionary monetary policy very difficult. An economy as large and complex as the American economy is not easily fine-tuned. That is increasingly the case as the international economy acquires more influence on domestic economic conditions.

A second tool the Fed can use to influence monetary policy is the **discount rate.** When the Fed was first established the discount rate was its primary tool for controlling money growth. Now it is used more to signal the direction of monetary policy than to effect actual changes in the money stock.

The Federal Reserve requires that banks hold a specified percentage of their deposits as **required reserves.** Required reserves may be held in the form of cash in the bank's vault (i.e., vault cash) or as a deposit at the Federal Reserve bank in its district. For example, Citibank may hold some of its required reserves in a reserve account at the New York Federal Reserve Bank. The amount of reserves any bank must hold is determined by the amount of deposits it holds and the **required reserve ratio,** which is set by the Federal Reserve Board.

As of September 1994, the required reserve ratio was 3 percent for depository institutions (i.e., banks, savings and loans, credit unions, etc.) with less than $51.9 million in checkable-type deposits and 10 percent for all checkable deposits in excess of $51.9 million.

When a bank's reserves are below the amount it is required to hold, it must make up the difference. One way that a bank can do this is to borrow additional reserves from the Federal Reserve bank in its district. This is called **discount window lending.** For example, Mellon Bank in Pittsburgh might request a loan from the Federal Reserve bank in Cleveland to make up a reserve shortfall. The interest rate charged on this loan is called the discount rate. Changes in the discount rate are traditionally initiated by the Federal Reserve banks and approved by the Federal Reserve Board. In the past the Fed used a low discount rate to encourage banks to borrow reserves and a high discount rate to discourage such borrowing. Like open-market purchases of Treasury securities, injections of funds made this way promote bank lending, which in turn increases the money supply. A high discount rate has the opposite effect.

Changes in the discount rate are infrequently used to change money-supply growth because it is not as powerful or precise a tool as open-market operations. To inject funds, the Fed must wait for banks to request loans, which forces the Fed to play a passive role in the conduct of monetary policy and actually encourages procyclical growth in the money supply that tends to strengthen both expansions and recessions.

Currently, the Fed's policy is to make discount window loans to banks at the discount rate only in special circumstances (e.g., seasonal credit shortfalls in agricultural banks). Routine needs for additional reserves to meet reserve requirements are commonly met in the **federal funds market.** Some banks may face reserve shortfalls; others will have excess reserves (i.e., more reserves than they are required to hold). Keep in mind that banks don't earn interest on their reserves, so banks with an excess can earn a profit by lending out their excess reserves overnight to banks with shortfalls. These loans are made in the federal funds market. The interest rate charged on these loans is called the **federal funds rate.** This interest rate is actually a more important indicator of monetary policy than the discount rate because it is highly sensitive to injections or withdrawals of reserves made through open-market operations, the Fed's primary policy tool.

The Fed's third policy tool is changes in the required reserve ratio. Congress gave the Federal Reserve Board power to alter the required reserve ratio in the 1930s. When the required reserve ratio is raised, banks must hold more of their deposits in the form of reserves and thus they have less money to lend out. Conversely, reductions in this ratio free up additional reserves that can be used to make loans and expand the money supply.

Unlike open-market operations and discount window lending, which affect only a handful of banks at a time, changes in the required reserve ratio affect every single bank, savings and loan, and credit union in the United States. Since small changes in this ratio can generate enormous changes in the money stock, this is a powerful policy tool. Because changes in the required reserve ratio are not useful for making minor changes in the money supply, however, this tool is rarely used.

As we've seen, control over the discount rate and required reserve ratio is ultimately vested in the Federal Reserve Board. But the most useful and most commonly used monetary policy tool, open-market operations, is guided by the deliberations of the FOMC. This suggests that the FOMC has become the primary force behind the determination of monetary policy. Here is a body of twelve voting members—none of whom is elected and only seven of whom are appointed by the president with the advice and consent of the Senate. The FOMC is part private, part public, largely independent of the legislative and executive branches, and it traditionally has deliberated entirely in secret. In our discussion of fiscal policy, we noted the intensity of the political forces that influence decisionmaking. But with monetary policy we have a powerful decisionmaking body that is isolated from the normal political pressures. How does it decide what to do?

Although it is true that the Fed, and the FOMC especially, are not subjected to the overt political influences that pervade other areas of economic policymaking, they are hardly insensitive to political realities. Members of the Fed are acutely aware of current economic conditions and their impacts. They are fully versed in the economic programs of the president, and they are well informed about congressional concerns. The chair of the Fed, for example, testifies frequently before congressional committees and thus has regular opportunities to hear what members of Congress have on their minds.

This is not to say that monetary policy decisions are the result of careful political calculations and compromises, as fiscal policy decisions often are. They are constrained by political realities in a broader sense. In fact, the Fed sometimes takes actions that anger presidents and members of Congress and becomes a scapegoat for politicians unhappy about economic conditions.

Charles L. Schultze, an economist who served as Lyndon Johnson's budget director and chair of Jimmy Carter's Council of Economic Advisers, has written, "In a pragmatic way, the Federal Reserve typically acts to reduce the chances of making serious mistakes by practicing a policy of 'leaning against the wind'" (Schultze, 1992: p. 187). When the economy seems to be expanding too rapidly or when the dangers of inflation rise, the Fed tends to tighten the money supply. When the economy is in recession, it may do the opposite. The Fed most often seeks economic stability by using monetary policy to counter other forces that seem to be destabilizing.

Microeconomic Policy

When it develops and implements fiscal or monetary policy, the federal government generally seeks to use its available instruments to bring about economic growth and prosperity. The focus is broad and the impacts are felt throughout much of the American economy. At other times, however, national policymakers initiate actions designed to affect a much narrower slice of the economy, often a single industry, sometimes a single company. We earlier described broad policy initiatives in fiscal and monetary policy as macroeconomic policy. These narrower undertakings are microeconomic policy.

Even though their focus is narrow, microeconomic policies sometimes have ripple effects through the entire economy. When the price of an important commodity such as natural gas is regulated at lower-than-market levels, for example, a wide spectrum of industries and consumers are able to operate less expensively than they could in the absence of regulation. That might allow industries to invest more and consumers to save more. It would encourage both to select natural gas as their fuel of choice rather than oil, coal, or some other fuel, thus affecting other fuel industries.

The American economy is tightly interconnected. Government intervention in one sector, even for the narrowest of purposes, can have indirect effects across a wide range of economic behavior. There are many types of microeconomic policy. Here we will focus on two of the most common, regulation and subsidies, and a third, industrial policy, which is emerging into greater prominence as America tries to redefine its role in the late-twentieth-century global economy.

Regulation

In some ways, government has always intervened in certain segments of the market. It made generous grants of land to help the railroads expand across the continent, developed roads and canals to encourage internal development, and sponsored or conducted research to improve the productivity and financial well-being of farmers. Most of these interventions resulted from government's ownership of natural resources—land, water, or minerals, for example—or from the need for a government to function as a referee in competing claims or in distributing rights and benefits.

A new pattern of government intervention occurred in 1887 with the passage of the Interstate Commerce Act. After the Civil War, many consumers— farmers especially—felt victimized by railroads that charged more for short hauls, where they had a monopoly, than on long hauls, where there was competition; granted rebates to large shippers; and speculated in land. Those consumers sought government regulation of the railroads to correct some of these practices. Even the railroads themselves found some relief in government intervention. Cutthroat competition and practices designed to destroy competition had left many railroads anxious for some external controls on the marketplace.

The supporters of the Interstate Commerce Act, like supporters of many subsequent interventions in the economy, argued that they were acting to preserve the free market, not to undermine it. They did not seek government ownership of the railroads, they noted; they only wanted a national railroad industry that provided competition that was in the best interests of consumers and producers.

To accomplish this objective, Congress established a new federal agency, the Interstate Commerce Commission (ICC), and delegated to it the authority to enforce "reasonable and just rates," to forbid anticompetitive practices, and to investigate complaints and issue rulings that could be enforced in court. The ICC was unlike any other agency at the time. It was a commission composed of five members, each serving seven-year terms. The members were appointed by the president with the advice and consent of the Senate, and the president designated the chair of the commission. The commission, however, was not an executive agency but an independent regulatory commission designed to function outside the close control of the president.

This was **vertical regulation.** A single government agency was responsible for broadly regulating activity in a single industry. Subsequent efforts at regulation followed this pattern. These commissions varied in their size and the terms of their members, but the essential model of multimember bodies with a measure of independence from the president and responsibility for a single industry remained the norm for almost a century.

Regulatory commissions conduct investigations, hold hearings, and issue rules and regulations detailing the proscriptions they place on the operations of the companies they regulate. The Federal Communications Commission, for example, controls the allocation of new radio and television station licenses. All licensees are required to operate in the public interest. Licenses are granted for a fixed period of time, at the end of which a licensee must apply for renewal. At that time, the FCC invites public comments on the performance of the licensee. If it finds that a licensee has failed to meet its obligation to use its license in the public interest, the FCC can refuse to renew the license and grant that station's radio or television frequency to someone else.

When a regulatory commission decides to issue new rules to govern the behavior of an industry, it must first publish those in draft form in a government publication called the *Federal Register*. Publication of the draft rules is followed by a "public comment period" of at least thirty days. During this time, anyone can comment on the draft rules. Not surprisingly, a large portion of the comments come from companies that will be affected by the new rules. After the public-comment period, the commission reviews the comments, amends its draft rules if it deems such amendments necessary, then publishes the rules in their final version in the *Federal Register*. At the end of each year, all new rules are codified in another government publication called the *Code of Federal Regulations*.

In practice, the independent regulatory commissions have a mixed record. Some of them have been highly effective regulators at some times. The Securities and Exchange Commission, for example, played a significant role in stabilizing America's financial markets in their recovery after the stock market crash in 1929. The Consumer Products Safety Commission has often been aggressive in identifying dangerous consumer products such as children's pajamas treated with flammable chemicals and hair dryers insulated with asbestos.

But many of the regulatory commissions have, at various times in their history, come under the sway of the industries they were designed to regulate. They have, in terms used by some of their critics, been "captured" by those industries. This occurs in several ways. One is the appointment, with the acquiescence of the president and relevant congressional committees, of regulators who are friendly to the industry. Another is the expenditure of significant sums by the industry to employ lobbyists and provide information to persuade the commission to see things in a light favorable to the industry. A third is through the operations of what are sometimes called "iron triangles"—mutually supportive relations among the regulatory commission, the congressional committees that oversee its work, and the regulated industry.

As a consequence of these political distortions of the regulatory process, regulation efforts have often failed to secure their primary objective of protecting consumers and ensuring competition in the marketplace. A commission called the Civil Aeronautics Board (CAB) existed from 1938 until the mid-1980s with responsibility for regulating the commercial airline industry. For the first forty years of its existence, not a single new commercial airline was certified to enter the passenger marketplace. Hence one of the principal outcomes of the work of the CAB was the protection of the airline companies it was designed to regulate.

In response to these failings of the approach to regulation initiated by the Interstate Commerce Act, two developments have occurred in recent decades. One is the development of a new pattern of **horizontal regulation,** or what some have called social (as contrasted with economic) regulation. Instead of a single agency regulating a single industry, as is the case for the FCC and the communications industry, a federal agency is assigned responsibility for regulating certain kinds of economic behavior across all industries. In the Civil Rights Act of 1964, Congress created the Equal Employment Opportunity Commission (EEOC) and charged it with ending discrimination in hiring based on race, color, religion, sex, or national origin. The EEOC's jurisdiction covers virtually every industry in the country. It is a multimember commission similar to the traditional regulatory commissions, but its jurisdiction is not confined to a single industry.

The Occupational Safety and Health Administration (OSHA) is another example of a federal agency with jurisdiction for specific economic behavior—in this case, workplace safety—across many industries. OSHA, however, is not a multimember commission. It is instead an agency within the Department of Labor and is headed by a single assistant secretary.

A second response to the inadequacies of old-style regulation has been a process of **deregulation.** In the late 1960s and early 1970s, a growing number of economists began to question the value of federal regulation. Often, they argued, the regulatory process was counterproductive. It reduced rather than enlarged competition and it benefited the regulated industries at the expense of consumers rather than vice versa. Some economists, and many industry executives, also argued that government regulation added significantly to the cost of doing business and thus reduced productivity and raised consumer prices, since companies passed on the cost of regulations to their customers.

These criticisms stimulated a movement for deregulation aimed at disengaging the federal government from some of its interventions in the market. Starting in 1978, important deregulation efforts occurred in natural gas prices and in the airline, banking, and railroad industries. The Reagan and Bush administrations cut back significantly as well on mine and general occupational safety and on environmental and cable television regulation.

Like regulation itself, deregulation has had mixed effects. Some consumers benefited from airline deregulation because it resulted in more flights and lower fares; others suffered a loss of easy access to air travel. Retrenchments in mine-safety inspection and regulation lowered the operating costs of mining companies but raised the risks for miners.

The contemporary free market is hardly free in the pure sense. There are few economic activities left that do not come under the purview of some federal agency. Although each act of regulation is targeted at a specific problem and is usually designed for limited purposes, the accumulation of all of this regulatory activity has a broad and potent impact on the national economy.

Subsidies and Credit Policy

The government intervenes in specific industries not merely to regulate behavior but also, in some cases, to encourage investment and to assist industries through hard times. It has two primary instruments for doing this: grants and loans. Grants are a transfer of cash from the government to some private entity for a specified purpose. The Agricultural Stabilization and Conservation Service in the Agriculture Department, for example, makes grants of cash to farmers to encourage them to take erodable land out of production. These farm subsidies, as they are called, have existed since the New Deal and are designed to help control the supply of agricultural produce that comes onto the market. By limiting supply, the federal government works with farmers to help maintain farm prices at a level high enough for more farmers to stay in business.

In some parts of the country in the 1990s, a major effort was under way to save important species of fish from overfishing. In the Atlantic, for example, the haddock stocks have dropped to dangerously low levels. To allow the haddock stock to replenish, the government has established tight limits on the haddock catch. Obviously, this threatens the livelihood of people in the fishing business who rely on haddock for their income. To help them through this period of reduced fishing—and, for them, of reduced income—the federal government has established a grant program that compensates fishers for some of their lost income.

The more common mechanism for subsidizing certain kinds of economic activities is federal credit policy. The federal government is the largest single creditor in the country. It lends more money and guarantees more loans than any other entity. Some of the federal government's credit activities involve direct loans. Programs are established that permit individuals or organizations to apply to the federal government for a loan. The government approves the applications and lends the money. The borrower repays the government directly. Farmers may borrow from the government under an array of programs. So may small businesses. So may homeowners victimized by floods or hurricanes.

More often, the government does not lend the money directly. Instead it guarantees loans made to individuals or corporations from private lending sources such as banks and mortgage companies. The government guarantees to the lender that the loan will be repaid even if the borrower defaults. This reduces the lender's risks and makes it easier for potential borrowers who might not normally meet the lender's standards to get a loan. Because the risk is greatly diminished when the government guarantees a loan, lenders' overall costs of covering bad loans are also reduced and they often provide loans at lower interest rates than would be the case without government intervention. In Chapter 2 we described the mortgage-loan guarantees provided to World War II veterans under the GI Bill. Those were an early example of this approach.

Loan guarantees are now widely used by the federal government both to encourage new investment and other kinds of economic behavior and sometimes to protect industries or companies in transition. The government guarantees loans to college students to permit more young people to attend college. It guarantees mortgage loans to many homeowners and other loans to many small businesses. In 1979, Chrysler, one of the country's leading automobile manufacturers and an employer of 130,000 American workers, was in danger of going broke. It turned to the federal government and asked for loan guarantees to permit it to restructure. There was much political debate about whether the federal government should provide loan guarantees to help Chrysler. Some economists argued that dying or sunset industries should be allowed to fail. That's how a free market works, they argued. Other employers would move in to fill the vacuum created by Chrysler's demise; its employees would find other jobs.

But other economists and most politicians argued that Chrysler was too big to die without some government effort to save it. This was another example of the classic dilemma of economic freedom versus economic security. As a practical matter, Chrysler had manufacturing facilities in many congressional districts, and the representatives of those districts were more interested in saving the jobs of their constituents than in slavish devotion to free market economics. So the government voted to provide Chrysler $1.5 billion in loan guarantees. Chrysler later returned to profitability. Federal intervention did, in fact, save the company and the jobs of many of its employees.

Credit subsidies have become an increasingly popular form of microeconomic policy. As Figure 3.6 indicates, the federal government's credit obligations have grown dramatically in recent years.

This is problematic in several ways. One is that credit policies are not subject to annual or systematic review in the way the budget is. When the federal government makes grants for microeconomic purposes, those grants go through the budget process and are subject to annual review. When the government provides loan guarantees, however, there is no similar mechanism to ensure accountability and to impose budgetary discipline. As a consequence, the federal government's loan obligations and costs have been growing rapidly with little control.

A second problem is that credit programs rarely derive from any broad or carefully developed macroeconomic policy. Each program is usually the

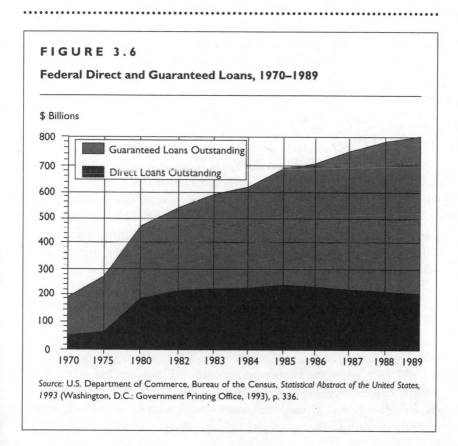

FIGURE 3.6

Federal Direct and Guaranteed Loans, 1970–1989

Source: U.S. Department of Commerce, Bureau of the Census, *Statistical Abstract of the United States, 1993* (Washington, D.C.: Government Printing Office, 1993), p. 336.

creation of a congressional committee seeking to help an industry, a company, or a group of individuals for political purposes. Members of Congress especially want to help their constituents or those groups that provide them with important financial support for their campaigns. One way to do that is to establish a credit program that provides loan guarantees to the favored group.

It is important to remember that direct grants and loans and loan guarantees are subsidies. They deploy the financial resources of the federal government to aid certain industries, companies, and individuals. By so doing, they favor one kind of economic behavior over another or one industry over its competitors. Had the federal government not intervened with loan guarantees to save Chrysler or the Lockheed aircraft company in 1971, those companies might have failed and their competitors might have benefited. Some economists argue that in a free market, efficient companies should survive and inefficient companies should fail. When the government intervenes to help failing companies, according to this view, it rewards inefficiency. But defenders of these and other interventions counterargue that credit policy is a valid way to encourage desired economic behavior, to stabilize markets such as the agricultural market, and to protect companies that are not suffering as much from their own inefficiency as from broader market forces or technological transitions.

Industrial Policy

A new form of microeconomic policy has been emerging in recent years and is likely to grow to greater prominence in the years ahead. This is **industrial policy,** the efforts of the federal government to identify strategic industries with high potential for growth and facilitate their emergence with protection from foreign competition and direct subsidies, especially for research and development.

The increasing interest in industrial policy is stirred largely by the rising prominence of the global economy at the end of the twentieth century. More and more, American companies are competing with foreign corporations in the domestic market. More and more, American companies are seeking markets abroad.

The problem is that many other countries have governments that participate in national economies even more directly than the American government does. In Japan, for example, the Ministry of International Trade and Industry (MITI) plays an important role in directing new research and investment for Japanese companies. In France, Canada, and many other countries, government subsidies help their corporations compete internationally.

In some cases, this leaves American companies at a competitive disadvantage. Companies themselves lack the resources to conduct the research and development necessary to compete in new fields with companies in foreign countries where research and development are often centralized and subsidized with government funds. This has accelerated the pressures on the federal government to develop an industrial policy that will help the American economy stay on the cutting edge of new technologies and manufacturing processes and compete effectively for new markets. President Clinton made it clear during his campaign in 1992 that he wanted the United States to move more aggressively in the development of an industrial policy. He intended, he said, to "create a civilian advanced technology agency . . . [to] sponsor civilian R&D and technology projects, create new jobs for scientists, technicians, and engineers, and develop and produce manufacturing expertise for state-of-the-art technologies and innovative new products" (Clinton and Gore, 1992: p. 78).

Early in his term, he initiated efforts to bring this about. The Advanced Technology Program was created to subsidize high-risk, high-technology research with broad economic potential. Several hundred million dollars were invested in the program. The Advanced Research Projects Agency (ARPA) in the Defense Department made similar investments in new technologies with both military and civilian uses. One example is the Clinton administration's commitment of more than $0.5 billion to accelerate the development of flat-panel display screens.

Industrial policy is not without its dangers, however. Industrial policy is intended to encourage and accelerate innovation. But it can have the opposite effect. When government invests in research and development of one technology, it chooses not to invest in others. The goal is to "pick winners." But there is real risk that government will not pick a winner but a loser, that the path government chooses to follow will not produce the most commercially viable processes or products and other countries will gain an advantage. Most new innovations have emerged from competition in the marketplace. One company developed the Beta videocassette-recording technology, another developed VHS, another developed laser discs. Consumers had a choice of technologies and made their decision. Had industrial policy been the source of funding for these developments, it is entirely possible that fewer options would have been explored, with a different outcome than the one that the market produced.

Supporters of industrial policy argue, however, that those risks are overstated. A sound industrial policy doesn't pick winners, it encourages competitive innovation. And, they argue, the real risk is not too narrow a focus for research and development but simply too little research and development because American companies cannot afford to compete on their own with the research and development supported by the industrial policies of other countries. If the American economy is to stay in the forefront, according to this view, it must have support from the government for innovation.

Trade Policy

To influence trade between the United States and other countries, decision-makers utilize policy tools to affect **exports** and **imports.** Exports are the dollar value of goods or services produced by U.S. residents and purchased by foreigners. These include American-made airplanes, wheat, and movies sold abroad. Imports are the dollar value of goods or services produced by foreigners and purchased by Americans. Imports include such items as German beer, Italian shoes, and Swiss chocolates sold in the United States.

Since the 1980s, policymakers have more carefully monitored the impacts of their decisions on the **trade balance,** which is computed as the difference between exports and imports. When imports exceed exports there is a **trade deficit.** In this case earnings from the sale of exports don't generate enough income to pay for all our imports. When exports exceed imports, there is a **trade surplus.** As Figure 3.7 indicates, American trade deficits have recently become the norm.

Instruments of Trade Policy

Many different tools are available to promote exports or limit imports. We discuss some of the most common.

Tariffs. A tariff is a tax on imported goods. Tariffs may be levied as a flat charge on each unit of an imported good (e.g., $3 per barrel of oil) or as a percentage of the imported good's value (e.g., 25 percent of the value of an imported truck). Tariffs are used to protect domestic producers of specific products from foreign competition by artificially raising the price of the foreign goods in U.S. markets. Because a tariff reduces competition, it benefits U.S. producers of protected goods and their employees. Less competition permits manufacturers to charge higher prices than they could in the absence of a tariff.

But what helps manufacturers harms consumers, who must pay higher prices for both the foreign and domestically produced good. Consider the case

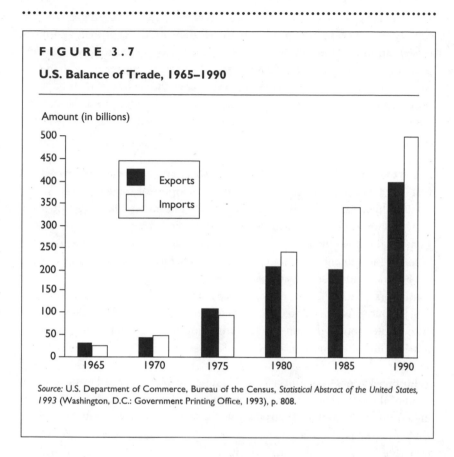

FIGURE 3.7

U.S. Balance of Trade, 1965–1990

Amount (in billions)

Legend: ■ Exports □ Imports

Source: U.S. Department of Commerce, Bureau of the Census, *Statistical Abstract of the United States, 1993* (Washington, D.C.: Government Printing Office, 1993), p. 808.

of automobiles. The hundreds of thousands of stockholders and employees of Chrysler, Ford, and General Motors benefit from tariffs placed on foreign cars and trucks, but the millions of people in the United States who buy cars or trucks are hurt by the higher price they must pay for their vehicles. Economists tend to believe that in most cases the economic costs of a tariff exceed the economic benefits. As tariffs have been reduced in the postwar period through a variety of free trade agreements, other forms of trade restraint have become more popular.

Export Subsidy. This is a payment to a domestic firm or individual selling goods abroad. An export subsidy may be a flat payment per unit shipped or it might be calculated as a percentage of the value of the exported good. Export subsidies are paid to help domestic producers compete in foreign markets. The subsidy permits domestic producers to sell their products abroad at a lower price than they could otherwise. This lowers the domestic supply of the exported good and thus forces U.S. consumers to pay a higher price than they would in the absence of the subsidy. In every case, the economic costs of an export subsidy exceed the economic benefits. Producers gain from the subsidy, but consumers are hurt by higher prices; the government collects no revenues but incurs costs.

Import Quotas. These are government restrictions on the amount of a good that may be imported. Because they limit the supply of foreign goods, quotas result in higher domestic prices for the affected products. Quotas produce the same economic effects as tariffs with one exception: They result in no revenue gains for the government. Instead, all of the profits from higher prices revert to both U.S. and foreign producers of the restricted good. In 1984, for example, the Federal Trade Commission estimated that U.S. sugar quotas cost domestic consumers $1.266 billion. This loss was partially offset by the $616 million that U.S. producers were able to collect by charging higher prices. Foreign producers benefited too, to the tune of $238 million transferred to them by U.S. consumers (Tarr and Morkre, 1984).

Voluntary Export Restraints (VERs). These are quotas applied by the government of the *exporting* country, usually at the request or demand of the importing country. In the late 1970s, as gasoline prices grew dramatically in the United States, Japanese automakers gained greater market shares. U.S. drivers were switching to smaller cars, which at that time were not manufactured in large numbers by U.S. automakers. As U.S. output of cars declined, political pressures mounted for some form of protection from Japanese competition. The federal government asked Japan to adopt voluntary export restraints. Fearing unilateral adoption of protectionist measures by the United States, Japan agreed to limit its exports in 1981. As predicted, the price of both Japanese- and American-built cars increased, with windfall profits earned by automakers in both countries.

For the purpose of computing costs and benefits, VERs are exactly like import quotas. In every case a tariff that would limit imports by a specified amount is economically preferable to a VER that limits imports by the same amount. Funds that would have been collected by the government under a tariff become windfall profits earned by foreigners under a VER. A study by the Federal Trade Commission found that about two-thirds of the costs of VERs, borne by domestic consumers of steel, automobiles, textiles, and apparel, is accounted for by windfall profits earned by foreigners (Tarr, 1989).

Local-Content Requirements. These regulations demand that some specified percentage of a retail product be produced domestically. These requirements benefit producers at the expense of consumers.

Red-Tape Barriers. These include health, safety, environmental, and customs procedures that are enacted for the sole purpose of placing enormous barriers on the import of goods. Many U.S. firms claim that Japan has effectively used such barriers to limit their access to Japanese markets. These barriers are an informal means of adopting quota restrictions and have the same costs and benefits.

The Politics of Trade Barriers

For each of these trade barriers, the costs to consumers almost always exceed the benefits to domestic producers and their employees. If this is so obvious, why do trade barriers prevail? The answer is that trade policy, like other areas of economic policymaking, is primarily the result of political interplay among special interests rather than a logical analysis of national welfare. Trade barriers are usually adopted to protect the income of specific interest groups.

Quotas on foreign-car imports are supported as necessary to protect the jobs of U.S. autoworkers. Assuming the goal is worthwhile, are we using the most efficient means to achieve it? A subsidy to firms that employ autoworkers would achieve the same goal and at the same time eliminate windfall profits for foreign automakers while reducing the price of cars for U.S. consumers. Some of the benefit of lower prices would be offset by higher taxes or reduced government outlays in other areas, which would be needed to finance the subsidies.

But this option isn't politically viable. Imagine trying to pass an employment subsidy through Congress. How could members justify their votes to preserve the jobs and *high wages* of autoworkers in this time of tight federal budgets? Although import quotas actually cost more than employment subsidies, quotas are politically more acceptable because the costs are less visible: They take the form of higher automobile prices rather than government outlays. In this case, as in many others, trade barriers are imposed because the public is unaware of the true costs of the restraints.

Other explanations for inconsistency in our use of trade barriers are political in nature. Sugar quotas impose large costs on U.S. citizens, but most Americans are unaware that there is a sugar quota or that it raises their cost of living. This is especially true because we purchase most of our sugar as an ingredient in other prepared products such as candy or cereal. And for most Americans, the annual cost of the sugar quota is relatively small, averaging about $5 per person. For individual sugar producers, however, the quota can be worth hundreds of thousands of dollars. Because of these cost differentials, sugar producers are allied in a special-interest group that successfully lobbies Congress.

In this case, as in most other cases of trade barriers, the benefits are heavily concentrated within a small group and the costs are widely dispersed. Special-interest politics thus ensure that trade barriers will be adopted even when they are clearly not in the national interest.

Moves Toward Free Trade

Although certain special interests fight to protect themselves from foreign competition, the general thrust of trade policy over the past half-century has been toward free trade. Since 1947 there have been eight major multilateral trade agreements conducted under the auspices of the **General Agreement on Tariffs and Trade** (GATT). The most recent round of negotiations, the Uruguay Round (so named because the negotiations that initiated it took place there) was approved in December 1993 by the 115 nations that are GATT signatories and later supported by the Congress in special session after the 1994 election.

Another important recent multilateral free trade agreement is the **North American Free Trade Agreement** (NAFTA). NAFTA was initially crafted to eliminate virtually all trade barriers between the United States, Canada, and Mexico over a fifteen-year period. This treaty was negotiated by the Bush administration, with side agreements governing environmental standards, labor standards, and import surcharges subsequently negotiated under President Clinton.

The fight over NAFTA clearly illustrates the importance of special-interest politics in the formulation of international trade policy. Like GATT, NAFTA required presidential and congressional approval, with the House vote proving to be NAFTA's greatest hurdle. Anti-NAFTA forces joined the battle first, launching an aggressive campaign to convince House members and their constituents that NAFTA's passage would cause the economic decline of the United States.

H. Ross Perot, a NAFTA foe, spoke of the "giant sucking sound" that he said would result from the movement of millions of U.S. jobs to Mexico. This argument, also articulated by most U.S. trade unions, presumed that as tariffs fell,

Many labor unions opposed NAFTA and other efforts to reduce trade and tariff barriers because they feared that American companies could operate more cheaply elsewhere and jobs would be lost in the United States. Reprinted courtesy of Dan Wasserman, *Boston Globe,* Los Angeles Times Syndicate.

U.S. firms would move production facilities south to take advantage of lower Mexican wages. Environmentalists and public interest groups battled NAFTA, arguing that U.S. firms would relocate to Mexico in order to escape expensive U.S. environmental and safety standards. They claimed that in order to keep jobs at home we would ultimately lower our own standards.

NAFTA proponents, led by President Clinton, tried to counter these emotional appeals with a barrage of facts. They pointed out that although the average Mexican wage was much lower than its U.S. counterpart, Mexican workers were much less productive and the infrastructure (i.e., roads, electrical grids, etc.) was much less developed. Mexican production might save money in hourly wage costs, but this savings would be more than offset by other costs of manufacturing in Mexico. This would limit job migration.

The critical House vote of November 17, 1993, was not as close as expected, with 234 members voting for NAFTA and 200 members voting against. President Clinton won the battle, but his chief weapon wasn't the logic of his arguments; it was pork. In order to build a majority coalition, concessions were made to wheat farmers living near the Canadian border, citrus and vegetable farmers in Florida, the textile industry, sugar producers, and others. Domestic and special-interest politics, more than objective economic analysis, accounted for NAFTA's victory in Congress.

Conclusion

This overview of economic policymaking reveals three broad and dominant characteristics. First, economic policymaking is decentralized and disjointed. Almost every agency of the executive branch and every committee of Congress has some role in making economic policy. Americans look to their presidents to be economic leaders, but presidents lack the authority, the resources, and the knowledge to control economic policymaking. They are powerful players in economic debates, but they must compete for influence with many other powerful players.

Second, economic policymaking is deeply and inevitably political. Americans are directly affected by the federal government's economic policies and they communicate their wishes and fears through every available channel. Economic decisions are made by political leaders, and they respond to political moods and political pressures. Spending is hard to cut because Americans enjoy the benefits they receive from government programs. Taxes are hard to raise because Americans hate to pay for what they get from government. Hence much of the turmoil and tension of economic policymaking results from torturous efforts to align political constraints with economic realities.

Third, policy changes slowly because change is so hard to effect. Each year's budget is only marginally different from the previous year's. Tax policy changes almost every year, but most of the changes are not broad departures from what has gone before. A large budget deficit, like the one that emerged in the 1980s, persists because of the political difficulty in shrinking it. Because there are so many policymakers trying to broker so many competing interests in an economy of great size and complexity, economic policy is resistant to radical alteration. Like a great ocean liner under full steam, the American economy is a powerful force. But it turns slowly.

4

....

Dilemmas of Contemporary Economic Policy

A society which is clamoring for choice, which is filled
with many articulate groups, each urging its own
brand of salvation, its own variety of economic
philosophy, will give each new generation no peace
until all have chosen or gone under, unable to bear the
conditions of choice. The stress is in our civilization.

—Margaret Mead

IN 1994 PRESIDENT CLINTON proposed a comprehensive program of welfare reform that attacked some of the causes of structural unemployment. Structural unemployment is an enduring plague of modern economic life. Traditional Keynesian policies of higher spending or lower taxes won't eliminate it; neither will monetarist prescriptions for stable money growth or supply-side proposals for tax cuts on corporate income. These policies target cyclical components of unemployment, not its endemic causes. To reduce structural unemployment, specific programs must reduce both disincentives to work and the skills deficiencies of the structurally unemployed.

To move welfare recipients into jobs, Clinton initially proposed to spend $9 billion over five years on education, training, and child care. In theory, education and training should impart job skills to the structurally unemployed (on welfare) and subsidized child care should eliminate work disincentives that result from a shortage of affordable day care. To comply with the Budget Enforcement Act of 1990, the new spending had to be obtained from an equal and specific increase in taxes, an equal reduction in other spending programs, or a combination of the two. Because raising taxes is politically difficult, Clinton proposed to fund this proposal mostly by reducing spending on other programs.

In the initial proposal, for example, $500 million was to be obtained by eliminating crop price-support payments to farmers who earn more than $100,000 annually in *nonfarm* income. The point of these cuts was not to end assistance to family farmers struggling to make a living in agriculture but to end what some have called "welfare for the wealthy." According to a Clinton adviser, "It's not cutting subsidies to farmers. It's cutting subsidies to doctors and lawyers who live on farms" (Seib, 1994: p. A20).

But this was not the first effort to cut federal subsidies for wealthy farmers, and as President Clinton soon learned, it is easier said than done. Agricultural interest groups quickly responded by dispatching their lobbyists to Capitol Hill to generate support among farm-state lawmakers for continuation of the subsidies. The lobbyists came armed with arguments about the benefits the subsidies provide and the costs of dismantling them. They argued, for example, that price-support payments might have a side effect of providing welfare for wealthy farmers, but their essential purpose is to stabilize both the supply and price of food in the United States. Without the subsidies, the lobbyists asserted, rich farmers would begin to plant as much of their land as possible, driving down food prices and causing severe economic hardships for smaller, poorer farmers. The result, they argued, would be a need for government to spend even more on subsidies. Both Democrats and Republicans on the House and Senate Agriculture Committees responded sympathetically to these arguments. The committees ignored presidential requests to stop the subsidies.

Is this a smart way to make public policy? Perhaps not. Presidential leadership often fails. Special interests often overwhelm the general interest. Subgovernments often dominate the center. Money talks. Most Americans believe that the federal government, particularly the president, has a responsibility to stabilize the economy. But most also believe that government programs often fail. Many economists and policy analysts share that view. What's wrong? How do we account for the widespread perception that economic policy is often ill designed or poorly executed?

In this chapter we offer some answers. We've already identified the central dilemma of economic policymaking as the struggle to balance economic freedom with economic security. Here we focus on some of the most important contemporary aspects of that dilemma: the political and economic constraints that complicate contemporary economic policymaking. It has never been easy to forge consensus or build majority coalitions for economic policy in the United States. It has never been harder to do so than it is now.

Constraints and Disagreements

Searching for the One True Model

Economists and policymakers use several different models to explain inflation, unemployment, real GDP growth, and other economic variables. But uncertainty prevails about which is the "true" macroeconomic model of the U.S. economy. As we note elsewhere, these models often deliver conflicting advice to decisionmakers regarding optimal policy choices. Keynesians assert that changes in the federal budget deficit should be used to minimize economic variability; monetarists argue for emphasis on stable money growth.

A policy failure resulting from poorly developed macroeconomic theory is illustrated by the 25 percent personal income tax cuts enacted by President Reagan in 1981. Supply-siders claimed that these cuts would generate a substantial increase in government revenues. The prediction was based on a supply-side economic theory illustrated by the **Laffer curve** depicted in Figure 4.1.

This theory asserts that if tax rates are zero percent, tax revenues will be zero, but as tax rates increase, revenues will increase up to a point. At the other extreme, if tax rates are 100 percent, tax revenues will be zero because no one will want to work. In theory, if the United States was at point A in Figure 4.1 , tax revenues could be *increased* from Y to X by reducing tax rates from A to B.

Unfortunately, our knowledge about intermediate points on the Laffer curve is incomplete, but policy outcomes critically depend on the missing information. Perhaps the "true" Laffer curve is the one in Figure 4.2. In that case a reduction in tax rates produces a small *decrease* in tax revenues. Between fiscal years 1982 and 1983, when much of the tax cut was phased in, individual income tax revenues declined from $297.7 billion to $288.9 billion.

Unexpected but lasting changes in relationships between macroeconomic variables create problems in predicting the likely impacts of any policy. Keynesians in the Kennedy and Johnson administrations formulated policy based on the assumption that there was a long-run negative trade-off between the

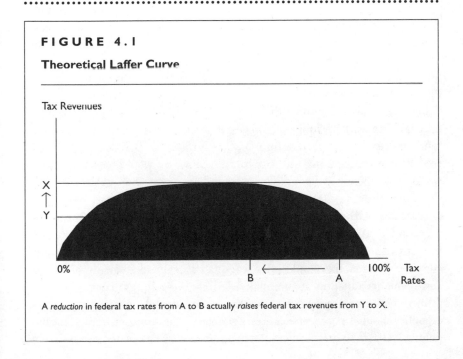

FIGURE 4.1

Theoretical Laffer Curve

Tax Revenues

X
↑
Y

0%   B   A   100%   Tax Rates

A *reduction* in federal tax rates from A to B actually *raises* federal tax revenues from Y to X.

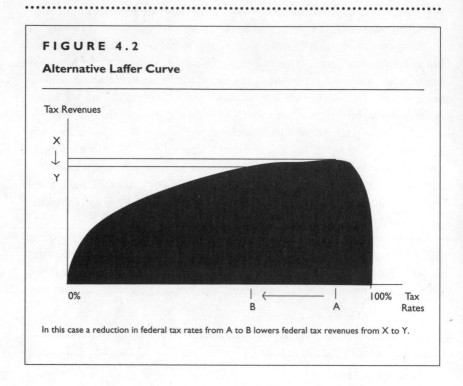

FIGURE 4.2

Alternative Laffer Curve

In this case a reduction in federal tax rates from A to B lowers federal tax revenues from X to Y.

inflation rate and the unemployment rate. This relationship, known as the **Phillips curve,** appears in Figure 4.3.

Keynesian theory assumed that unexpected inflation could be used to induce labor to work for lower real wages. If you expected inflation to be 3 percent next year, you might ask for a 3 percent raise. But if actual inflation exceeded your expectations and rose to 5 percent, you would be unexpectedly working for a lower real wage. The more inflation exceeded workers' expectations, the greater the decline in unemployment as firms increased their hiring of labor that had become *relatively* less costly. According to this theory the only decision for policymakers was which combination of unemployment and inflation to choose from the possible combinations on the long-run Phillips curve. At point A, they could offer workers lower unemployment, but at the cost of higher inflation. At point B, a low rate of inflation is achieved, but through higher unemployment. Early Keynesians argued that expansionary fiscal policy should be used when necessary to move the economy from point B to point A—that is, to reduce unemployment by inducing an increase in inflation.

FIGURE 4.3

Traditional Keynesian Long-Run Phillips Curve

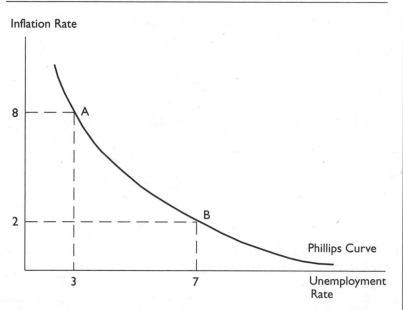

There is a negative tradeoff between inflation and unemployment in the long-run. An increase in the inflation rate from 2 percent to 8 percent lowers the unemployment rate from 7 percent to 3 percent.

Although the Phillips curve in Figure 4.3 appeared to explain the relationship between unemployment and inflation during the 1960s and early 1970s, that relationship seemed to have changed by the mid-1970s. Workers became hypersensitive to rising inflation and its effects on their purchasing power, and this appeared to alter the shape of the Phillips curve over the long run. The current relationship is better described by the **natural rate hypothesis,** which suggests there are no long-run trade-offs. Phillips curves such as the one in Figure 4.3 are now believed to describe only short-run relationships between inflation and unemployment. Expansionary macroeconomic policy might temporarily reduce the unemployment rate below the natural rate, but the long-run consequences of this would be higher inflation with no reductions in unemployment.

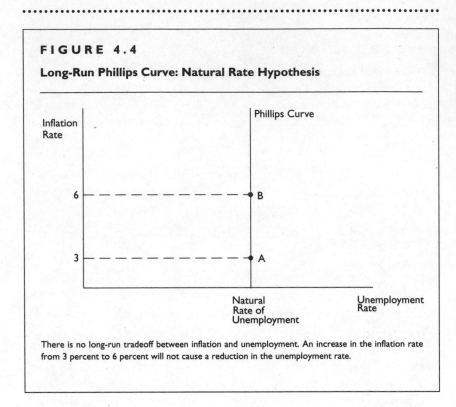

FIGURE 4.4

Long-Run Phillips Curve: Natural Rate Hypothesis

There is no long-run tradeoff between inflation and unemployment. An increase in the inflation rate from 3 percent to 6 percent will not cause a reduction in the unemployment rate.

The theoretical, long-run Phillips curve indicated by the natural rate hypothesis appears in Figure 4.4. Point A represents the economy's initial inflation and unemployment rates; and point B represents the long-run consequences of an expansionary fiscal policy: higher inflation but no reduction in unemployment. The natural rate hypothesis depicted here suggests that Keynesian approaches are doomed to fail. The contemporary economy does not meet their traditional assumptions about the long-run relationship between inflation and unemployment. The search for the one true model continues.

Uncertainty: Indicators and the Business Cycle

Contemporary policy formulation is also complicated by the inability of decisionmakers to precisely know the macroeconomy's current condition. This problem, known as **recognition lag,** results from the technical difficulties of collecting timely data on the economy's performance. Key measures of performance such as the unemployment rate, inflation rate, and rate of real output growth are used by economists to determine the economy's position in the business cycle. Because collecting, compiling, and analyzing data take time, government statisticians won't know this month's unemployment rate until about one week after the month's end. Real GDP growth and broader measures of inflation are only available quarterly, with fairly accurate estimates unavailable until three months past the end of a quarter. So reliable data on economic growth during January through March isn't available until sometime in June.

The problem of assessing the current state of the economy is compounded by the need of policymakers to see a trend in the economic data before concluding that a change has occurred. For example, a sudden sharp decrease in real GDP growth might signal the beginning of a recession. But it might also represent a temporary deviation from an expansion caused by a major flood, hurricane, or blizzard.

The difficulties in determining the economy's vitality in "real time" are illustrated by the National Bureau of Economic Research (NBER) Business Cycle Dating Committee's experience in pinpointing the beginning and end of the 1990–1991 recession. It wasn't until spring 1991 that enough economic data accumulated to permit the committee to pinpoint the recession's onset in July 1990. The following recovery was so anemic that dating the end of the recession was even more difficult. By December 1992, the NBER had sufficient data to show a clear trend of economic recovery and put the date of the end of the recession at March 1991, over a year and a half earlier.

Mechanisms that relate changes in fiscal or monetary policy to changes in economic variables don't function systematically. So when macroeconomic policy options are evaluated, decisionmakers don't know precisely how much time will elapse before any policy change begins to affect the economy. Economists estimate that anywhere between six months and two years must pass before a policy change will have its full impact on the economy. These lags are long and variable, so it is impossible to know beforehand whether a policy change will be felt sooner or later.[1]

Because fiscal and monetary policy appear to operate with a minimum lag of six months, and because of problems stemming from recognition lags, some argue that formulating policy based on currently available data is analogous to driving a car while looking in the rearview mirror—with the same consequences for the economy! To overcome these difficulties, it would seem logical to formulate policy based on economic forecasts of where the economy will be over a planning horizon six months to two years ahead.

The FOMC tried to do this when it began to raise short-term interest rates in February 1994. Specifically, economic indicators showed a potential for inflation growth late in 1994 or in 1995. Because of lag effects, the FOMC responded by raising interest rates *before* actual data reflected a trend of rising inflation. Many in Congress responded angrily, demanding that the FOMC wait until inflation was clearly a problem. Senator Paul Sarbanes, Representatives Henry Gonzalez and Kweisi Mfume, and others predicted that rising interest rates following from the FOMC's actions would cause a recession.

In reality, only time will tell if the FOMC's switch to a less expansionary monetary policy was prudent. But an analysis of the forecast accuracy of Federal Reserve staff predictions and the predictions of private economic forecasters found that forecast errors for total output growth are so big that forecasters generally cannot determine, in either the current quarter or a year in advance, whether the economy will be expanding or contracting. Thus there is a good chance that discretionary fiscal or monetary policy based on forecasts won't stabilize the economy because policy is likely to be formulated to solve problems that won't arise (Meltzer, 1987).

Uncoordinated Macroeconomic Policies

An important difficulty in predicting how a policy will affect the economy results from the lack of any formal mechanisms to coordinate domestic fiscal and monetary policy and to coordinate American macroeconomic policies with those of foreign trading partners. Decisionmakers often assume that policy alternatives will be implemented in a favorable economic climate, but this isn't always the case. In 1981, President Reagan enacted an expansionary fiscal policy partially in the form of tax cuts aimed at substantially increasing business investment in new machines and equipment. During the policy-formulation stage, the administration forecast that this policy would dramatically stimulate economic growth. But the policy was implemented during a period of extremely contractionary monetary policy that generated prime interest rates above 20 percent. Monetary and fiscal policy conflicted, and investment did not increase as predicted.

In 1993, both fiscal and monetary policy were expansionary. But many U.S. trading partners, including Germany and France, were pursuing more contractionary macroeconomic policies. This limited European demand for U.S. exports. Because exports contribute positively to U.S. GDP, and because exports are an increasing portion of GDP, macroeconomic policies abroad can significantly affect unemployment, inflation, and economic growth in the United

....

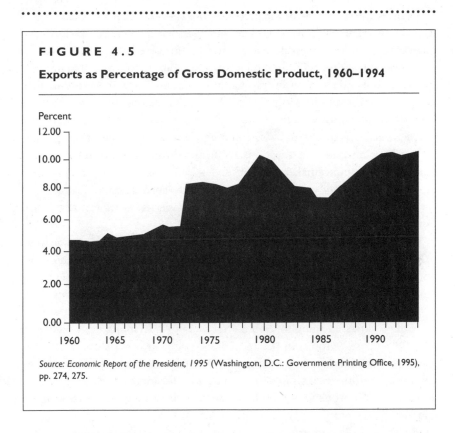

FIGURE 4.5

Exports as Percentage of Gross Domestic Product, 1960–1994

Source: *Economic Report of the President, 1995* (Washington, D.C.: Government Printing Office, 1995), pp. 274, 275.

States. Figure 4.5 illustrates how exports have increased as a percentage of GDP. With the 1993 passage of the North American Free Trade Agreement (NAFTA) and the 1994 approval of the General Agreement on Tariffs and Trade (GATT), exports are likely to become even more important, and changes in macroeconomic conditions abroad will have even larger impacts on the American economy.

Communications Overload

American citizens, as individuals and in groups, have never had greater access to their elected policymakers. Nor have policymakers ever had greater access to citizens.

Yet improved communications have not markedly improved policymaking. Better communications should clearly inform policymakers regarding voter preferences, satisfying one of the preconditions for rational policymaking. But it hasn't always worked that way. The messages that policymakers receive are often contradictory. Americans want better-funded programs but lower taxes. They want cuts in "wasteful" spending (usually meaning spending that benefits someone else) and increases in "productive" spending (meaning spending that benefits them). They don't want inflation or high unemployment, but they do want steady economic growth.

Policymaking is contorted by loud and unrelenting communications pulling and pushing in conflicting directions. As the opportunities for communication have improved, policymakers—especially elected officials—have become hypersensitive to public opinion. Conflicting messages, powerfully communicated and sensitively received, have led to policy inertia, or what many critics now call gridlock.

The contemporary economic-policy landscape is more crowded than ever before. The crowding is caused not simply by more government agencies and legislative committees with economic responsibilities, though there are certainly plenty of those. The largest addition to the sum of participants involved in economic policymaking is the rapid proliferation of special-interest groups since the 1960s. According to the *Encyclopedia of Associations,* the number of organized interest groups in the United States grew from 10,298 in 1968 to 20,643 in 1988. An unprecedented array of special-interest groups now seeks to communicate the desires of their respective—and increasingly narrow and specialized—constituencies to both elected officials and those charged with the conduct of regulatory policy.

In 1993 and 1994, for example, an insurance industry trade group ran a series of widely noted TV and radio advertisements that featured a fictional couple, Harry and Louise, who complained that the president's health care reform proposals would limit their ability to obtain medical treatment and to obtain it from the doctor of their choice. This media campaign received much credit for reducing the level of voter support for dramatic reforms.

Some special-interest groups have mastered the use of new technologies to generate, overnight, thousands of letters and faxes from voters directing their senators or representative how to vote on critical legislation. Individual meetings between members of Congress and lobbyists working for business, labor, trade, or professional associations are also used to communicate the views of specific interests. **Political action committees (PACs),** the political arms of special-interest groups, make campaign contributions to incumbents and challengers who are sympathetic to—or well positioned to help accomplish—an interest group's objectives.

MAY WE CUT IN.... AGAIN!!

Republicans and Democrats have both sought to cut federal spending in the 1990s, but they have not often agreed on the specific programs and the amounts that should be cut. Reprinted courtesy of *The Boston Globe*.

Special-interest groups closely monitor the *Federal Register* to learn of proposed rule changes, and they communicate their members' views to the appropriate regulatory agency during the comment period. Lobbyists for the group submit written responses to proposed changes, draft alternative rules more favorable to their members, and appear at agency hearings to make their views known. If these approaches fail, litigation may be used to force an agency to modify a rule. Finally, special interests can attempt to persuade Congress to override an agency's approach to regulation by lobbying for a change in the agency's legal mandate or a reduction in its budget (particularly for enforcement).

The result of the interactions of special-interest groups on different sides of an issue is often economic policy based less on what is best for the economy than what best serves the special interests of powerful groups. This is not a recipe for rational, coherent, or predictable economic policy.

The Incremental Character of Policy Change

Often, especially in the construction of the federal budget, attempts to pursue rational policymaking are foiled by the powerful force of incrementalism. Current economic policy becomes a continuation of past policy with only minor changes. Inertia subverts change.

Political interests and political processes account for the strong tendency toward incrementalism in economic policymaking. Sometimes it's politically expedient to make only minor changes in policy in order to reduce conflict and potential stalemate that would arise from making major changes. Changes in Congress's organizational structure during the 1970s dramatically decentralized power in that institution. This atomization of power has produced 535 legislators more loyal to their own constituencies than to their party leaders. The building of majority coalitions is more difficult than it was, and legislative gridlock often results.

President Clinton faced this problem in 1993 when trying to pass his deficit-reduction bill. Even though both chambers of Congress were controlled by the president's party, he had to promise many special favors to members in order to win their votes and avoid gridlock. Clinton promised Representative Marjorie Margolies-Mezvinsky, whose critical vote we discussed earlier, that he would come to her district and personally run a forum on entitlement reform. Clinton earned Senator Bob Kerrey's vote when he promised to appoint Kerrey to chair a new commission on entitlement reform. Ultimately, the president's plan passed, but by 218 to 216 in the House and only after Vice President Gore cast a tie-breaking vote in the Senate.

Incrementalism is stronger than ever in the Senate because of changes made recently in the use of the filibuster. In order to prevent all Senate business from being put on hold during a filibuster, a two-track system was created whereby an announced filibuster could continue on one track while other business proceeded on a second, independent track. Filibusters under the new procedures delay, sometimes permanently, the legislation at which they're specifically directed. The costs of staging a filibuster are now so low that filibusters are more common. During the 102d Congress in 1991–1992, twice as many filibusters were staged as in the entire nineteenth century, when only sixteen filibusters occurred (Calmes, 1994: p. A14).

Because the Senate schedule is so full, just the threat of a filibuster can keep a bill from coming to the floor. Consequently, on controversial issues, the real majority required to pass legislation is not the fifty-one needed to win a floor vote but rather the sixty votes needed to stop a filibuster. The size of this Senate hurdle favors incremental policies because they are less controversial and thus less likely to be blocked by a filibuster.

This is illustrated in the 1994 congressional debates over health care reform. The reform proposal offered by President Clinton would have required a massive restructuring of what amounts to 14 percent of the U.S. economy. Powerful political forces, in and out of Congress, mounted in opposition. Even the leaders of the Democratic majority in Congress could not construct a significant reform measure that could win a majority in both houses. Big changes are harder to effect than small changes, and Clinton's health care proposal was a big change indeed.

Incremental change is also a characteristic of economic policymaking because current congressional operations—multiple committee assignments, large and overlapping committee jurisdictions, and tight scheduling of floor debate, for example—discourage meaningful discussion of different policy options and inhibit consensus building. The election of Republican majorities to both houses of Congress in 1994 was accompanied by promises to break the legislative gridlock on Capitol Hill. House Republicans pledged to fulfill their Contract with America in the first hundred days of the 100th Congress. On some measures, they did indeed move swiftly and sweepingly. But on the most complex and radical changes in economic policy—a balanced-budget amendment, deep tax cuts, entitlement reform, and spending reductions—the new Congress found consensus more elusive. Even in the afterglow of significant electoral turnover in 1994, dramatic changes in economic policy were hard to effect.

Uncertainty about economic models and about current and future changes in the business cycle also inspire an incremental approach to policy change. Lack of knowledge is a primary reason behind the FOMC's incremental changes in monetary policy during 1994. By February 1994 many signs—short-term real interest rates roughly equal to zero, high rates of real GDP growth, unemployment rates close to the natural rate of unemployment—suggested that prospects for higher inflation in late 1994 or early 1995 were rising. The FOMC concluded that it should switch from the expansionary monetary policy, adopted to fight the recession of 1990–1991, to a more neutral monetary policy.

Because of the uncertainties and the high economic costs of erring too much on either side, however, the FOMC adopted a policy of incrementalism. Specifically, the federal funds rate was raised from 3 to 5.5 percent in six steps between February and November, with monthly increases of 0.25 percent in February, March, and April and 0.50 percent in May and August, followed by a 0.75 percent increase in November. During this period, the Fed continued to monitor indicators of future inflation as well as data on unemployment and GDP growth in an attempt to assess the most recently adopted interest-rate hikes and to determine any need for further increases. On August 16, 1994, Chairman Alan Greenspan said that the Fed would continue to monitor the economy, "but these actions are expected to be sufficient, at least for a time, to meet the objective of sustained, non-inflationary growth" (Thomas, 1994: p. A14).

The Contemporary Monsters of Economic Policy

Some constraints impose such significant roadblocks to the pursuit of rational economic policy that they loom as monsters over the policymaking process. We discuss three of them here: the entitlement monster, the pork-barrel monster, and the deficit monster.

The Entitlement Monster

A major constraint on any significant restructuring of the federal budget is the vast portion of federal spending that is committed to entitlement programs. **Entitlements** are commitments made by the government to provide certain kinds of benefits permanently. They do not require annual action because entitlements are based on permanent authorizations and appropriations. For example, federal law mandates that any veteran who served more than 180 days on active duty in the armed forces is entitled to veterans benefits (including education, mortgage subsidy, health care). When a qualified veteran applies for one of these benefits, the government is required to provide it because the veteran is legally entitled to it. The annual cost of these entitlements is determined not by some fixed amount authorized and appropriated by Congress but by adding up the costs of all benefits provided to all veterans who apply for them in a particular year.

The primary categories of mandatory entitlement spending are (1) *social insurance programs* such as Social Security, railroad retirement, unemployment compensation, veterans compensation and benefits, and agriculture price supports; (2) *government health insurance programs* including Medicare for the elderly and disabled and Medicaid for the poor; (3) *government pensions* for retired civilian and military employees; and (4) *means-tested programs* to aid the poor such as Supplemental Security Income, Aid to Families with Dependent Children (AFDC), and food stamps.

Some analysts call this "uncontrollable spending" because it is not subject to the normal disciplines of the appropriations process. Over the past half-century, entitlements have become a popular form of federal benefit program. They are pleasing to the recipients who do not have to plead with Congress or the president every year to maintain or increase their benefits. Those benefits are guaranteed by law. They are popular with legislators because they provide valuable benefits to constituents but do not require annual legislative battles over the maintenance or magnitudes of the programs.

A macroeconomic benefit of entitlement programs stems from their role as

automatic fiscal stabilizers. For example, during recessions, more people qualify and apply for programs such as AFDC, food stamps, and Medicaid. Government spending rises automatically, which tends to limit the depth of the recession, helping to stabilize the economy. During economic expansions fewer people qualify for means-tested entitlement programs, government spending automatically declines, and the inflationary pressures of the expansion are diminished. Economists have estimated that the macroeconomic stabilizing properties of entitlement programs are significant. Table 4.1 identifies some of the largest entitlement programs in the federal budget for FY 1994.

TABLE 4.1

Selected Entitlement Programs in the Federal Budget, Fiscal 1994

Program	Actual 1994 Expenditures (in $ billions)
Means-tested programs:	
Medicaid	82
Food stamps	25
Supplemental security income	24
Family support	17
Veterans' pensions	3
Child nutrition	7
Earned income tax credit	11
Student loans	3
Other	3
TOTAL	177
Non-means-tested programs:	
Social Security	317
Medicare	160
Other retirement and disability	72
Unemployment compensation	26
Veterans' benefits	18
Farm price supports	10
Social services	6
Net of others	4
TOTAL	612
TOTAL, Mandatory Spending	789

Source: Congressional Budget Office, *Reducing The Deficit: Spending and Revenue Options* (Washington, D.C.: Government Printing Office, 1995), p. 224. Totals are slightly affected by rounding.

To further strengthen these entitlement programs, Congress often "indexes" benefit levels. **Indexing** is designed to protect benefit levels from the impact of inflation. If, for example, you were a Social Security recipient and the benefit payment you received each month from the Social Security administration remained the same year after year, your real income would steadily decline because of inflation. A dollar received this year would purchase less than a dollar received last year in a period of inflation.

To maintain the value of entitlement benefits like Social Security, Congress has tied benefit levels to some measure of inflation, usually the consumer price index; hence the term "indexing." When the index changes, benefits do as well. This annual change is called a cost-of-living adjustment (COLA). So in a time of inflation, benefit levels increase so that beneficiaries suffer no loss of purchasing power.

Over time, the combination of a growing array of entitlement programs beyond the control of the annual appropriations process and the steadily increasing pressure of benefit levels indexed for inflation has produced a dramatic upward surge in (1) the percentage of federal expenditures committed to entitlement programs and (2) the overall level of federal spending. COLAs, in particular, have exacerbated the problem. The federal government calculates COLAs based on increases in the consumer price index (CPI), which for many reasons tends to overstate the actual rate of inflation. Alan Greenspan, chairman of the Federal Reserve Board, has testified that the CPI may overestimate inflation in any given year by as much as 0.5 to 1.5 percent. This may not sound like much of a discrepancy, but combined with the compounding effects of annual COLA adjustments, it is partially responsible for the huge surge in entitlement spending since the 1970s. Greenspan estimates that if we continue to use current, upwardly biased methods of indexing, the budget deficit over a five-year period will be $150 billion higher than it would have been otherwise (Greenspan, 1995).[2] Figure 4.6 indicates recent and projected growth of mandatory spending as a percentage of GDP.

Efforts to reduce entitlements are always emotionally charged and highly political. This has been especially true with programs that benefit the elderly. Powerful interest groups such as the American Association of Retired Persons and the National Committee to Preserve Social Security and Medicare are potent defenders of these programs. Whenever a challenge occurs, they can be counted upon to wage an intense battle on the airwaves and in the halls of Congress to prevent any reductions in benefits.

Congress has occasionally reduced the cost of an entitlement program by holding down cost-of-living adjustments, capping payments to providers of

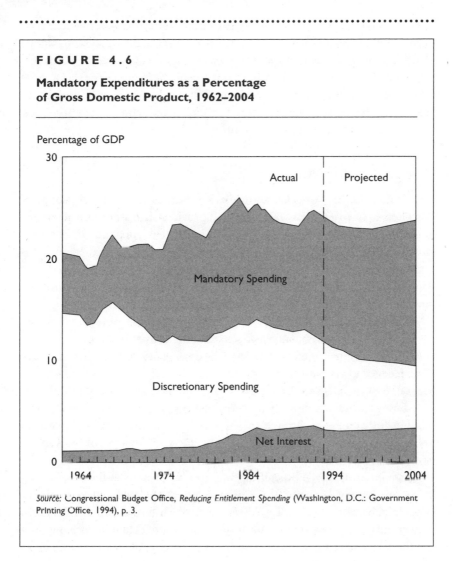

FIGURE 4.6

Mandatory Expenditures as a Percentage of Gross Domestic Product, 1962–2004

Percentage of GDP

Actual | Projected

Mandatory Spending

Discretionary Spending

Net Interest

Source: Congressional Budget Office, *Reducing Entitlement Spending* (Washington, D.C.: Government Printing Office, 1994), p. 3.

medical care, or restricting eligibility for benefits. But these are rare events with little more than marginal impacts on the costs of entitlements. Where it has acted at all, Congress has generally been able only to slow the future growth in entitlements, not to kill or shrink existing programs.

Entitlements survive and grow because of their broad political support. The average value of those entitlement benefits for the families that receive them is

$10,320 (in 1990 dollars). Almost half of all American families benefit from some entitlement program. Although almost everyone is opposed to budget deficits, almost no one wants to cut an entitlement program from which they benefit to help balance the budget (Congressional Budget Office, 1994: p. x). The intensity of the defenders of any specific entitlement program almost always overwhelms the general interest in deficit reduction. The entitlement monster is enormous. It is hard to control, nearly impossible to slay.

The Pork-Barrel Monster

The House Public Works Committee is the largest committee in Congress. Members fight to get seats on it because it provides such an extraordinary opportunity to direct federal funds to the districts they represent. You can drive down the Bud Shuster Highway near Altoona, Pennsylvania (named after Rep. Bud Shuster, R–Pa.) or visit the new federal courthouses in the districts of Rep. James Traficant (D–Ohio) and Rep. Jimmy Duncan (R–Tenn.). All three are members of the Public Works Committee.

Or if you really want to see the federal government at work, you can visit West Virginia. West Virginia's senior senator, Robert Byrd, was chair of the Senate Appropriations Committee from 1989 through 1994. Early in his tenure, Byrd pledged to his constituents that he would funnel a billion dollars worth of federal projects into West Virginia in five years; it actually took him only two. The booty included a new FBI fingerprint lab worth $185 million and $149 million for a highway through the Appalachian Mountains. Only when he sought to move the entire CIA headquarters to West Virginia did Byrd appear to be overreaching.

These kinds of federal expenditures on specific projects in the states or districts of individual members of Congress are called **pork-barrel spending.** Most members believe there are electoral benefits in "bringing home the pork." Voters will reelect them, they think, if they can use their clout in Washington to get the jobs and economic development possibilities that result from a major federal expenditure in their district. Farmers in flood-threatened districts want flood-control levees. Shipbuilders in coastal districts want navy contracts to build new warships. Small businesses in remote rural districts want new highways to connect them to larger markets. The federal government spends funds for all these purposes and many more. And there is fierce competition among members to get their share of the funding for these special projects, "to bring home the pork."

The competition to obtain these projects is an upward pressure on overall federal spending. One way to get a majority to support a pork-barrel spending bill is to include enough projects in it for a majority of the members. Many members are critical of this kind of often wasteful spending, but most also understand the political benefits of getting some of it for the people they represent.

Efforts to curb such spending rarely get very far because they are overwhelmed by the powerful demands of special-interest groups and the political survival instincts of members themselves. Rep. Tim Penny (D–Minn.) retired from the House in disgust in 1994. "This is how the system works," he said: "You help me; I help you. I don't blow the whistle on your pork; you don't blow the whistle on mine" (Pound and Pasternak, 1994: p. 43).

The Deficit Monster

Ross Perot transformed the deficit into a major campaign and public policy issue in 1992. Producing and starring in thirty- and sixty-minute televised "infomercials," he argued forcefully that large and rising deficits would reduce U.S. productivity and drown future generations in a sea of debt. President Clinton adopted much of the Perot argument when he scrapped his proposed middle-class tax cut and made deficit reduction the centerpiece of his 1993 fiscal policy proposals.

The current pattern of large annual budget deficits began in the 1970s, as illustrated earlier in Figure 1.6. During this time the deficit rose significantly during recessions and fell during expansions, but the subsequent decline never equaled the prior increase. The fact that the United States continued to run larger and larger deficits during vigorous economic expansions suggests that the size of the structural budget deficit was rising. In fact, during this period entitlement programs initiated as part of President Johnson's Great Society began to require larger and larger budget outlays. These outlays were not offset by equivalent declines in discretionary spending and were only partially offset by rising tax receipts.

The recessions of the early 1980s produced further increases in the budget deficit. An extremely robust recovery began at the end of 1982 (i.e., FY 1983), but still the annual budget deficit remained in the $200 billion range. The primary source of these unprecedented deficits was the combination of President Reagan's 1981 tax cuts, large increases in defense spending, and steadily rising entitlement expenditures. Toward the end of the decade, the budget deficit declined into the $150 billion range, in part due to a series of "revenue enhancers" (i.e., tax increases) enacted on the recommendation of President Reagan. By 1990, however, the deficit was again soaring to new heights. This time the proximate causes were the recession of 1990–1991 and the costs associated with the crisis in the savings and loan industry.

The deficit has been growing for a quarter-century, but it took years to become a policy issue. That is not surprising: The benefits of deficit spending tend to occur in the short run, and the costs are not fully realized for many years. Keynesians aggressively promoted the short-run benefits of deficit spending, so these are well known by the public and Congress. Benefits include fiscal stimulus of the macroeconomy, which, through increases in aggregate demand for output, may produce *temporary* reductions in unemployment and higher rates of economic growth.

Those who argue that the large deficits of the 1980s and 1990s are not problematic note that, adjusted for inflation, the deficits incurred since Fiscal 1982 are still smaller than those generated during World War II. Figure 4.7 illustrates changes in the *real* budget deficit.

But the spike in the deficit during World War II was a temporary phenomenon undertaken for a specific and widely supported purpose: to win the war. Today's deficits, although currently lower in real terms than the World War II deficits, are part of a rising trend in deficit spending that shows no signs of abating. Large, rising, and enduring deficits impose major costs on society. Consider the following:

1. To the extent that large budget deficits produce large increases in aggregate demand not offset by less expansionary monetary policy, inflation may increase as growth in aggregate demand outstrips growth in aggregate supply.
2. Large deficits add to the national debt, resulting in an ever larger government demand for credit to finance new deficits and to refund previously issued debt. This produces an increase in the overall credit demand of government. Generally, this higher demand will cause an increase in interest rates that reduces business and individual access to credit.[3] In the credit markets, the federal government's need to borrow heavily crowds out private-sector borrowers. In the case of businesses, the result is less investment in equipment and machinery.

   Unless government borrowing is solely for the purpose of financing public investments such as new highways, bridges, and seaports, deficits will produce a lower rate of growth in the nation's capital stock than would otherwise occur. Labor productivity will be lower than it could

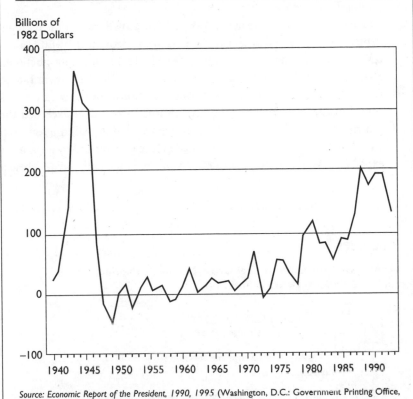

FIGURE 4.7

Real Federal Budget Deficits, Fiscal Years 1940–1994

Billions of
1982 Dollars

Source: Economic Report of the President, 1990, 1995 (Washington, D.C.: Government Printing Office, 1990, 1995), pp. 296, 383 (1990); 276, 277, 299, 365 (1995).

have been and standards of living will improve at a slower rate, if at all.

3. The amount of crowding out can be reduced by inflows of credit from foreigners who purchase U.S. Treasury securities as well as stocks and bonds issued by U.S. corporations seeking to finance purchases of machinery and equipment. During the 1980s, foreign savings provided a significant source of credit for the United States. By 1993, in fact, nearly

20 percent of federal debt was owed to foreign investors (*Economic Report of the President, 1994:* p. 370). But excessive reliance on foreign savings is worrisome because it necessitates that American macroeconomic policy focus increasingly on the concerns of foreign creditors in order to maintain credit inflows, potentially at the expense of domestic macroeconomic concerns.

4. As long as the growth rate in GDP exceeds the growth rate of the national debt, a country should be able to meet its future debt burden without necessitating lower standards of living. As Figure 4.8 illustrates, between 1947 and 1981 the growth rate in real GDP exceeded the growth rate in real debt, with a few exceptions during recessions.[4] But this pattern reversed in the early 1980s as the growth rate in real debt exceeded the growth rate in real GDP and remained higher even though the recession ended in 1982 and the rest of the decade was characterized by a vigorous expansion. Although the growth rate in GDP and the national debt began

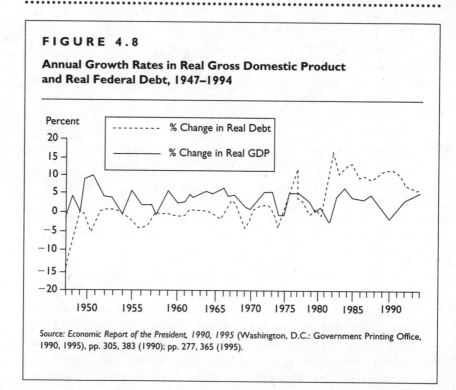

FIGURE 4.8

Annual Growth Rates in Real Gross Domestic Product and Real Federal Debt, 1947–1994

Source: *Economic Report of the President, 1990, 1995* (Washington, D.C.: Government Printing Office, 1990, 1995), pp. 305, 383 (1990); pp. 277, 365 (1995).

to converge in 1994, this is a temporary phenomenon resulting from unusually high and unsustainable GDP growth. In the long run, if debt continues to grow faster than GDP, America's public debt burden will exceed the government's ability to meet its financial obligations.

5. Large and growing budget deficits limit current and future flexibility in fiscal policy. By the end of 1991, President Bush felt compelled by the apparent weakness of the economy to engage in expansionary fiscal policy. When the president's economic advisers began a full exploration of policy options they quickly discovered their options were severely limited by a decade of large budget deficits and forecasts of even higher deficits to come. There was a fear that proposals bold enough to expand the economy would raise the deficit to record levels of close to $400 billion. At these levels, many expected the financial markets to respond immediately to projected higher future demands for credit by raising long-term interest rates. Higher rates could be expected to reduce business investment just as government was trying to increase it. In the president's attempt to stimulate the economy without raising the deficit, he included in many of his proposals *temporary* tax cuts and shifts in spending to earlier in the year.

Future limitations will occur as demographic changes (e.g., the aging of the baby boom generation, longer life expectancies, etc.), health care cost inflation, and assured benefit levels of entitlement programs require increased federal spending. Without changes in policy, by 2012 mandatory spending will rise from roughly 75 to 100 percent of government revenues. The amounts available for discretionary spending on programs such as defense, education, and environmental regulation will be increasingly limited (Bipartisan Commission on Entitlement and Tax Reform, 1994).

Another way to put the U.S. deficit in perspective is to make an international comparison. Figure 4.9 shows federal budget deficits as a percentage of GDP for Germany, the United Kingdom, the United States, Italy, and Japan. By this measure the deficits of Italy and the U.K. are substantially larger, and we can observe the costs of those deficits in terms of lower productivity in both countries. In contrast, Germany, and Japan in particular, are more fiscally conservative than the United States, as illustrated by their smaller deficits as a percentage of GDP. It is no coincidence that both countries have experienced productivity growth rates that are the envy of most of the world. Unless policymakers implement significant deficit-reduction measures, the U.S. experience

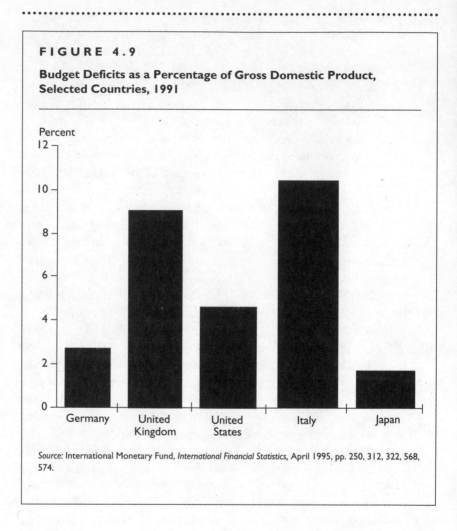

FIGURE 4.9

Budget Deficits as a Percentage of Gross Domestic Product, Selected Countries, 1991

Source: International Monetary Fund, *International Financial Statistics,* April 1995, pp. 250, 312, 322, 568, 574.

will in the future more closely resemble that of the U.K. or Italy than Germany or Japan.

How to Slay the Deficit Monster

The enormous accumulation of federal deficits in the last two decades of the twentieth century is the major roadblock to rational economic policymaking in our time. Several policy options have been proposed for putting the deficit on a downward course. Here we describe the most common of those.

Utilize Spending Caps

Spending caps are congressionally imposed limits to discretionary federal spending. As enacted by the Budget Enforcement Act of 1990, spending caps applied to three separate categories of spending; defense, international, and domestic. The Omnibus Budget Reconciliation Act of 1993 specified spending caps only for total discretionary outlays. Bills or amendments that mandate spending in excess of the caps are subject to points of order in the Senate and are prevented from reaching the House floor by the Rules Committee. The caps may be violated only if a recession is forecast or if an emergency is declared by the president and Congress (e.g., the Los Angeles earthquakes of 1994).

Spending caps will not bring about significant deficit reduction because they apply only to discretionary spending, which is not the primary cause of the long-run deficit problem. The amount of savings possible from this option is limited. As we noted previously, mandatory spending is expected to equal 100 percent of revenues by 2012. After that, all discretionary spending will add to the deficit. But even if Congress adopted draconian spending caps that eliminated all discretionary spending, after 2012 the deficit would still continue to rise at unsustainable rates as entitlement spending continued to rise faster than government revenues.

Reduce Defense Spending

Deep cuts in defense spending were adopted as part of the 1990 budget agreement and were not reversed by President Clinton. In fact, between 1990 and 1995, real defense spending fell from $264 billion to $209 billion. This option also falls well short of what is needed to address the long-run deficit problem. Even if defense spending were reduced to zero—a proposal that no one is making—the amount of savings achieved would be insufficient to offset the dramatic increases in entitlement spending that will begin in 1998.

Increase Tax Revenues

Tax revenues can be increased in two ways. Higher tax rates can be applied to individuals or groups already subject to taxes. Or the tax base can be expanded by levying new taxes on individuals or groups. Increasing the tax rates or expanding the tax base will not solve the deficit problem because growth in entitlements is expected to exceed growth in the tax base. Current projections are that the national debt will continue to grow at faster rates than GDP. Thus large increases in taxes cannot solve the problem because growth in tax revenues

An accumulation of large budget deficits during the Reagan and Bush administrations led some advocates to call for new—but politically unpopular—taxes to close the budget gap. Reprinted by permission of KAL, Cartoonists & Writers Syndicate.

(necessary to finance spending) cannot exceed growth in income forever. The government cannot tax people more than 100 percent of their income! A second problem with this option is that higher taxes create disincentives to work that will eventually choke off economic growth.

Grow Our Way Out

Theoretically, the expected future growth rate in the national debt would be sustainable if it were lower than the growth rate in GDP. Rather than focus on options that would lower future deficits and thus the growth rate in the debt, some argue that we should focus on options that would raise current levels of GDP growth. Although this option is theoretically possible, in reality the American economy cannot grow its way out of the problem because growth rates in the debt are so high. The level of GDP growth necessary to solve the deficit problem is generally not achievable for any sustained period.

Cut Entitlement Spending by Reducing Future Benefits

The primary source of the long-run deficit problem is runaway entitlement spending. For example, federal spending on health care grew at average rates of

10 percent during the 1988–1995 period and is expected to increase from 3.3 percent of GDP in 1994 to 11 percent of GDP by 2030, assuming that current benefits levels are maintained. But even if health care costs grew at the same rate as GDP, the aging of the population would still cause a doubling in spending for Medicare and Medicaid as a percentage of GDP.

To address the problem of rising entitlement expenses directly, the government must either reduce the level of benefits payable to future recipients or limit the eligible population or both. For example, Peter Peterson, a member of the Bipartisan Commission on Entitlement and Tax Reform, and Ross Perot have proposed that wealthy senior citizens with income over a specified amount not receive Social Security benefits. This would change Social Security into a means-tested program that would pay benefits only to individuals with a demonstrable need for supplemental retirement income. Plans to raise the Social Security retirement age early in the next century could be expanded to raise the retirement age even further in future years. If we assume that life expectancies won't increase dramatically, this measure would reduce the number of years the average individual would be able to collect Social Security benefits and increase the number of years he or she pays Social Security taxes.

Plans to reduce government spending on health care by capping payments to doctors and hospitals will not be effective. Doctors have been refusing to accept patients with Medicare because current government fee caps do not cover their costs. Additional caps would only reduce patient coverage further. Doctors and hospitals have also responded to the caps by raising the fees they charge other patients. To the extent that this occurs, the non-Medicare patients are paying an implicit tax to finance the health care of senior citizens. To reduce federal health care expenses significantly, Medicare benefits will have to be limited or the age at which individuals are covered will have to be raised.

Conclusion

In this chapter we have explored some of the major dilemmas and constraints in contemporary economic policymaking. Efforts to rationalize and coordinate policy decisions are handicapped by disagreement among economists and practitioners about economic theory. Which theory or model best describes the operations of the American economy? That's a question that stimulates more debate than agreement. And the absence of theoretical consensus is a major contributor to inconsistent and ineffective policymaking.

Policymaking suffers as well from economic indicators that often fail to clarify the current state of the business cycle. In economics, like marine navigation, it is hard to plot a course without knowing where you are, yet that is precisely the burden that economic policymakers must often bear. They are unsure where to head next because they are uncertain about where the economy is now.

In the absence of theoretical and analytical consensus, policymakers too often go off in opposite, conflicting directions. Fiscal policy is expansionary when monetary policy is contractionary, or vice versa. The American political system lacks consistently effective mechanisms for coordinating fiscal policy across all the institutions and policymakers who participate in it. Sometimes they work together; sometimes they do not. Nothing guarantees consistency or coordination in what they do.

The character of contemporary politics further burdens economic decision-making by providing few filters or screens for the multitude of communications generated by a robust and diverse society. In America, everyone has a stake and an interest in economic policy, and there are many ways in which to communicate concerns. Policymakers often find it hard to act—and especially hard to act boldly—in the face of so many communications demanding so many different responses to economic conditions. Congress, in particular, is afflicted with a procedural gridlock that results significantly from the number and intensity of special-interest concerns it must aggregate to get anything done. The communications overload too often results in inaction or inadequate action in the face of economic necessity.

Economic-policy decisions are powerfully constrained by three contemporary and unyielding "monsters." One is the momentum of decades of accumulation and growth of mandatory entitlement programs that provide benefits that fall outside the normal disciplines of the annual appropriations process. Another is the pork-barrel monster, which provides a flow of economic benefits to individual states and congressional districts that, like overeaters faced with a rich chocolate desert, they are unable to spurn despite knowing that they should. A third monster, bred in part by the other two, is the federal budget deficit. The deficit is now the central topic of national economic debate and the single largest influence on national budget decisions.

All of these constraints impose an incremental style on economic policy-making. Bold economic changes are nearly impossible politically and financially. So we rarely move far from current patterns of activity. What we can do tomorrow is usually a marginal variant on what we are doing today. Political limitations, in particular, tend to produce slow and incremental responses to economic problems and result from awkward procedures and the decentralization of power within Congress, and from the growing multitude of special-interest groups, each working full time to protect its members' interests.

5

....

Looking to the Future

Money is better than poverty, if only for financial reasons.

—Woody Allen

SUPPOSE THAT current medical technology and current entitlement programs had been available over 100 years ago. The leather-harness shop owner we encountered in Chapter 3 would have led a very different life. If he had fought in the Civil War and army doctors had determined that a gunshot wound had left him with even a small but significant disability, he would have been granted a medical retirement from the military. This would have entitled him to collect a pension equal to a percentage of his army salary until the day he died. If he had lived until sixty-five he could have retired, sold his business, and collected monthly Social Security checks—even if the sale of his shop had earned him $20 million. If, following his retirement, the shop owner had gotten very ill and required expensive medical care, most of his bills would have been paid by Medicare even if he had enough money to pay the full cost himself.

These entitlement programs, like many others, benefit the wealthy as well as the needy. In fact, only about $1 out of every $8 in entitlement spending provides assistance to individuals with incomes below the poverty level. In 1991 about one-quarter of all federal entitlement spending benefited individuals living in households with incomes over $50,000 (Peterson, 1993: p. 104). With an aging population and rising costs of health care due to advances in medical technology, we look to the future and ask: What impacts will such generous entitlement programs have on the budget deficit and the American economy?

The answer is plenty. Huge annual budget deficits are the single most prominent fact of contemporary economic policy, and uncontrolled entitlement expenditures are the primary cause of those deficits. To the naked eye, it seems that reducing budget deficits by reining in entitlement spending ought to be the central objective of future economic policy.

But a primary lesson of this book is that controlling entitlement spending (or raising revenues to pay for it) is not simple—not economically and certainly not politically. Economic-policy and budget questions now dominate the center of the American political agenda. They provide the substance for much of the contemporary political debate. The intensity of that debate has been especially aggravated by divided government—the presidency and the

Congress controlled by different political parties—a phenomenon that occurred in twenty-two of the twenty-eight years between 1969 and 1996.

In the 1994 elections, House Republican candidates sought greater leverage in this ongoing conflict over economic policy by generating a campaign document called the Contract with America. Not surprisingly, most of the key elements of that contract were economic promises, including a balanced-budget amendment, the line-item veto, welfare reform, tax relief, changes in Social Security, and reductions in regulations.

The historical American consensus on economic policy has been broad. Americans support capitalism and a vague conception of the free market. Within that broad consensus, however, there has always been ample room for debate about the meaning of capitalism and the operational details of the free market. That debate has always infused American politics and frequently structured the primary cleavages between the political parties. The central dilemma— economic freedom versus economic security—has long dominated the American political agenda.

What will this mean for the future? What outcomes are possible as Americans continue to struggle into the twenty-first century with issues that confound them at the end of the twentieth? In this chapter we explore three future scenarios for American economic policymaking. Scenario 1 assumes politics as usual with growing entitlement spending, no significant increases in revenues, constant and large budget deficits, and an expanding federal debt. Scenario 2 assumes significant reform of economic policy driven by a shared commitment to tame the entitlement, pork-barrel, and deficit monsters. Scenario 3 assumes that policymakers muddle through, making regular annual adjustments but not threatening the political status quo any more than is necessary to avert near-term economic disaster.

Scenario 1: Politics as Usual

In Chapter 4 we indicated that the deficit problem results from rapidly rising entitlement spending and cannot be eliminated through tax increases alone— even if tax increases were politically attractive—because projected entitlement spending (assuming current benefit levels) will grow faster than GDP. What does the future look like if inflation-adjusted entitlement benefits are not reduced or limited to smaller segments of the population?

First, the American standard of living will barely rise, and discretionary funds for programs that add to the quality of life (e.g., the National Park Service, the National Endowment for the Arts, the Corporation for Public Broadcasting, federal aid for undergraduate and graduate education) will shrink. This will happen as rising deficits crowd out the private investment that generates productivity increases that raise our real incomes and thus our standard of living. Rising levels of mandatory federal spending will increasingly crowd out discretionary spending.

Real interest rates will rise as the deficit increases from less than 3 percent of GDP today to more than 20 percent of GDP twenty-five years from now— when today's college students are in their prime working years. As a result, it will be increasingly difficult to borrow the money to buy a home or new car. Individual savings used to finance the federal deficit plus consumer and business demands for credit currently amount to about 5 percent of GDP. Individual savings of 5 percent minus government deficits of 3 percent yields 2 percent of private savings that is now available for consumer and business credit needs. But as federal deficits begin to exceed private savings around the turn of the century, interest rates will have to rise, either to attract a sufficient amount of foreign savings to finance the federal deficit or to induce U.S. citizens to save more.

The Social Security program illustrates the long-term problem. Most Americans think of their Social Security as earnings on the money they have saved over a lifetime by having Social Security premiums deducted from their paychecks in the form of FICA taxes. Not so. Social Security checks paid to today's retirees are funded primarily by the payroll taxes of today's workers. In fact, the Congressional Research Service has estimated that the average worker and spouse earn back everything they ever paid into Social Security, with interest, within four years of retiring (Thomas, 1994: p. A14).[1]

Today there are about five working-age people paying Social Security taxes for every retired person receiving Social Security benefits. But current projections suggest that in 2030, when most of the baby boom generation will have retired, there will be fewer than three working-age people for each person over sixty-five. At current tax rates the Social Security Trust Fund is projected to run out of money in 2029 (Bipartisan Commission on Entitlement and Tax Reform, 1994). Only significant increases in Social Security taxes or significant alterations in qualifications for and size of Social Security benefits can prevent that bankruptcy from occurring.

Every trend predicts that the cost of health care will become increasingly more expensive. This will result from a combination of government funding schemes for Medicare and the aging of the American population over the next half-century. In an attempt to slow the rate of increase in Medicare spending in the early 1980s, the government began to set **fee caps** on what it would pay for a wide range of medical services delivered under the Medicare program. Typically, the government's fee cap is well below the doctor's or hospital's charges. For example, Medicare pays only $5,703.71 for a hospital to treat a patient with a specific kind of heart attack.[2] Typical hospital charges for this treatment may exceed the government's reimbursement by $10,000 or more. In cases where hospital charges exceed Medicare fee caps, the hospital is not paid for the balance.

Since hospitals can't afford to provide health services at fees below cost, many hospitals have responded to government fee caps by charging non-Medicare patients higher fees—particularly those patients with more generous private health insurance plans. This is called **cost-shifting.** Typically, health insurance companies pass higher health care costs on to their customers in the form of higher premiums. Those with private health insurance usually pay the bill for cost-shifting. As the baby boom generation becomes eligible for Medicare in 2012, Medicare outlays will begin to soar. As larger and larger segments of the population qualify for Medicare coverage, the pressures on hospitals and other health care providers to engage in cost-shifting will increase.

In addition to bearing the increased burden of cost-shifting, working people will probably pay higher Medicare taxes. The Medicare Hospital Insurance Trust Fund is projected to run out of money by 2001 (Bipartisan Commission on Entitlement and Tax Reform, 1994). And total government spending on Medicare and Medicaid is projected to increase from 3.3 percent of GDP to 11 percent of GDP by 2030. Thus additional revenues will have to be raised to pay for these promised benefits.

We have indicated throughout this book that economic-policy change is hard to accomplish because the proponents of the status quo have great leverage in American politics. Those who benefit from current policies fight fiercely to retain their benefits and to control their costs. But the status quo—in economics and politics—is not a promising course for a healthy economic future.

If current economic policies remain in effect without significant change, most Americans will see their after-tax incomes shrink and their standard of living decline. Young people, on average, will have less disposable income than their parents and greater difficulty borrowing funds for the large expenditures they cannot afford out-of-pocket. Furthermore, the generous levels of government benefits available today through both discretionary spending and entitlement spending will almost certainly diminish in the twenty-first century.

Scenario 2: Significant Reform

What would significant reform look like? Proposals have been offered by a number of individuals and groups, including the Concord Coalition, the Bipartisan Commission on Entitlement and Tax Reform (BCETR), H. Ross Perot, and others. Most proposals recognize that the deficit problem is far too large to be solved solely by increasing taxes on the rich. Consider this: To achieve a balanced budget over the six years between 1994 and 2000 by taxing the "rich," we would need to confiscate 100 percent of the income of everyone with more than $175,000 in adjusted, pretax income. Alternatively, we could achieve the same goal by doubling the income taxes of every person with incomes of $50,000 or more (Peterson, 1993: pp. 29–30). "Taxing the rich" is a slogan with some populist appeal in political campaigns, but it's not a realistic solution to current economic problems. Instead, a combination of approaches will be required. Some of the most important recommendations follow.

1. *Require that all federal entitlements (except pensions for retired government employees) be gradually reduced for all families with incomes at some amount over the national median.*[3] Therefore, families who earn less would keep more of their entitlements and families that earn more would give up more. No poor person would lose a cent of federal benefits. Peter Peterson, president of the Concord Coalition and a member of the BCETR, has proposed that every family with an income of $35,000 or less be able to keep 100 percent of its entitlement benefits. Suggested benefit reductions for families earning more than $40,000 a year appear in Table 5.1. Income levels could be indexed to inflation so that real benefit reductions remain constant over time.

2. *Accelerate currently planned increases in the Social Security retirement age.* Following recommendations of the 1983 Commission on Social Security Reform, the retirement age will be increased from sixty-five to sixty-six in 2009 and to sixty-seven in 2027. The "normal" retirement age was set at sixty-five when the Social Security system was set up in 1935. Since then, of course, life expectancies have steadily increased. Reformers suggest that current benefit levels cannot be sustained when so many people live so many years beyond sixty-five. They propose to gradually move the eligibility age back even further and faster than the 1983 amendments. One plan would start raising the Social Security retirement age in 1995, by just three months per year, until the retirement age reached sixty-eight in 2006 (Peterson, 1993: p. 279).

3. *Raise Medicare premiums and copayments.* Medicare premiums were originally set to cover 50 percent of the program's costs. Currently, premiums cover

● ●

TABLE 5.1

Suggested Entitlement Benefit Reductions

Family Income	Average Benefit Reduction Per Family	Percent of Benefits Withheld
$40,000–$50,000	$910	5.2
$50,000–$75,000	$2,310	12.4
$75,000–$100,000	$4,520	24.3
$100,000–$200,000	$8,050	40.0
$200,000 and up	$15,345	71.5

Source: Adapted from Peter Peterson, *Facing Up* (New York: Simon and Schuster, 1993), p. 275.

only 25 percent of the costs. By raising premiums to cover 30 percent of the costs and by modestly increasing copayments (the portion of the bill paid by the patient), additional revenues would be raised. But more important, as people become personally responsible for more of the cost of their health care they become much more cost conscious about the care they demand. This would further limit future increases in Medicare spending.

4. *Limit the favorable tax treatment for employer-provided health insurance.* In World War II, when wages were frozen by the government, firms began to provide free or subsidized health insurance for their employees as a way to increase compensation without increasing wages. Because these benefits are not taxed as regular wage income, the federal government is subsidizing the purchase (through lost tax revenues) of health insurance by all families who receive this employer-provided benefit. Because people with larger incomes are taxed at higher rates, this subsidy gives the biggest tax breaks to the richest Americans. Limiting the tax exclusion only to employer-paid health plans that are of average cost or below would substantially increase government revenues.

5. *Raise the gasoline tax by 50 cents per gallon over a five-year period.* This proposal was supported by Ross Perot in the 1992 presidential election campaign. He argued that the tax would have two major benefits. It would increase revenues to help balance the budget and, by raising the cost of gasoline, it would increase incentives to conserve energy.

These are a sample of the kinds of proposals that have been offered to reduce the budget deficit. If a significant portion of them were put into effect, the budget deficit would dramatically decline and funds available for private investment in new capital, technology, and worker training would dramatically increase. Many economists believe that a better-educated workforce, more capital, and the technological breakthroughs bound to result from increased business spending on research and development would produce larger average annual increases in real GDP than we have experienced since 1973. This would permit standards of living to rise at the rate they did in the early postwar period.

Is everybody for this? Clearly not. A 1994 *Wall Street Journal*/NBC poll found that when Americans were asked if specific programs such as Social Security, Medicare, Medicaid, and farm subsidies should be cut, 66 percent said no even though 61 percent favored the general approach of cutting entitlements to reduce the deficit (Thomas, 1994: p. A14). The economic solutions are not so hard to identify. But in the eyes of politicians who hate to vote for benefit reductions or tax increases, the political path to those solutions is hard to navigate. Economic rationality clashes with political rationality. Significant reform of economic policies could tame the deficit monster. But the political will to enact such reform is in short supply.

Scenario 3: Muddling Through

In seeking to avoid both the certain economic disaster of politics as usual and the likely political suicide of significant economic-policy reform, policymakers might instead adopt a series of incremental, short-term measures. These temporary fixes wouldn't cure the endemic maladies of current economic policy, but they would keep disaster at bay for a while longer. This, in fact, is what President Clinton did in his 1993 deficit-*reduction* package. Among other changes, this five-year plan reduced defense spending, increased gasoline taxes, increased income taxes for the richest Americans, and slightly reduced the *growth rate* in entitlement spending.

Most incremental policy changes focus on reducing the growth rate in entitlements rather than eliminating or significantly reducing entitlement benefits or eligibility. Incremental changes can reduce the deficit and thus slow the growth rate in the federal debt. The 1983 Social Security reforms saved the system from a near-bankruptcy experience. But they accomplished little more than was minimally necessary to avoid disaster. The long-term outlook for the Social Security system remains bleak. The political difficulty in doing more than muddling through looms large.

One of the great but often unrecognized (by the public, at least) costs of con-. tinuing large budget deficits is their downward pull on productivity and economic growth. Incremental tinkering is not enough to restore high levels of productivity gains or to dramatically reduce the growth rate of the debt and perhaps even pay some of it off. To keep the debt from increasing, the government must reduce the deficit to zero. To reduce the debt, the government must run budget surpluses so that excess revenues can be used to pay off holders of U.S. government securities. Incremental change is unlikely to achieve such goals.

Nor will muddling through be enough to eliminate the burgeoning effects of demographic change on next century's entitlement spending. These changes will come in a rush after the turn of the century; their magnitude will overwhelm incremental or tepid responses. Successfully meeting them requires planning, not simple faith in the quick fix. When the chorus of baby boomers begin to demand the pensions and health care to which they think a lifetime of tax payments entitles them, the politics of postponement will drown in the din.

Conclusion

The entitlement monster is the critical macroeconomic problem that will confront policymakers over the next decade or more. Americans might respond to that by seeking to maintain the status quo of high benefits and low taxes, by seeking to achieve significant deficit reduction through major alterations of economic policy, or by muddling through from crisis to crisis.

The simple lesson of this book is that economic policy is shaped and confined by economic politics. The federal government has grown over the course of the twentieth century to be the single most important participant in the American economy. But in the final decades of the century, the government has lost much of its capacity to plot and steer a steady course, to use the instruments of economic policymaking to pursue coherent and rational objectives.

In the years ahead all Americans will confront the consequences of this. We hope the readers of this book have learned something about the nature and magnitude of the challenge that lies ahead and something that will help them to meet it successfully.

Discussion Questions

Chapter 1

1. Explain the differences between a command economy and a free market economy. Why do some countries have the former and some the latter?
2. Where in the business cycle is the U.S. economy currently located? How can you tell?
3. What are the principal signs of a strong American economy?
4. What are the principal ways in which the Keynesians and the monetarists differ in their explanations of how an economy operates?

Chapter 2

1. Are there consistent trends and beliefs that run through American economic policymaking in the twentieth century? If so, what are they, and how do you account for their endurance?
2. What are the most important turning points in the development of American economic policy over the past century? What significant changes did they yield?
3. What principal factors drove the expansion of the government role in the American economy?
4. What has been the relationship between economic theory and economic policy in twentieth-century America?

Chapter 3

1. In what ways is the appropriations process different from the process by which tax policy is made?
2. How would you characterize the relationship between the president and the Congress in contemporary economic policymaking?

3. Where does the Federal Reserve Board fit into national economic policymaking? How independent is it? How powerful is it?

4. In what ways does public opinion affect national economic policymaking?

Chapter 4

1. Who is to blame for the extraordinary growth in federal budget deficits in the past two decades?

2. What do you regard as the most feasible way to reduce the federal budget deficit?

3. Why did the federal government begin to create entitlement programs?

4. Should entitlements be maintained as a mechanism for distributing federal benefits to individuals or should some other mechanism replace them?

5. Of the future scenarios described in this chapter, which do you think is most likely to occur and why?

Chapter 5

1. Is it possible, in the current political environment, to bring about significant reform of the economic policymaking process? What are the principal impediments to that?

2. What are the major threats now facing the American economy?

3. What price will American citizens pay if there are no significant changes in economic policy over the next three decades?

4. What clues does the historical review in Chapter 2 provide about the possibilities for economic-policy change in the future?

Glossary

Appropriations. Formal congressional determinations of the amount and purpose of specific types of government spending.

Automatic Fiscal Stabilizer. Fiscal policy designed to have a countercyclical effect on the economy. A government program that provides for increases in spending without congressional action during recessions and for decreases during expansions. Also, a tax that produces proportionately more revenues during expansions and proportionately less revenues during recessions.

Balanced-Budget Amendment. A proposed amendment to the Constitution that would prohibit planned deficit spending except in times of national emergency.

Budget Authority. Money that agencies are authorized to spend, usually over several years, once an appropriation has become law.

Budget Deficit. The amount by which government expenditures exceed government revenues (derived from taxes, tariffs, and fees).

Budget Examiners. Employees of the Office of Management and Budget who review the annual budget requests submitted by government agencies.

Budget Surplus. The amount by which government revenues (derived from taxes, tariffs, and fees) exceed government expenditures.

Business Cycle. A period of time when economic growth is alternately above and below the economy's average rate of economic growth.

Capital. Includes factories, office buildings, warehouses, machinery, equipment, roads, and other durable goods used in the production of output.

Capital Gain. The profit earned by an individual investor who sells a previously purchased asset at a price higher than the original price.

College of Cardinals. A pseudonym for the chairs of the House appropriations subcommittees; given because of the chairs' prominence in the budget process.

Command Economy. An economy structured so that the government determines both the amounts and kinds of goods and services that are produced, the methods of production utilized, and the prices that will be charged for each good and service.

Concurrent Resolution on the Budget. An expression of congressional opinion, without the force of law, that provides guidance to the appropriations and tax committees on targets for revenues, new budget authority, outlays, the size of the deficit, the national debt, and federal credit activities.

Consumer Price Index (CPI). A measure of aggregate prices based on the weighted average prices of almost 400 categories of goods and services purchased by the typical consumer household.

Consumption. Total purchases of final goods and services by individuals for themselves or another person.

Continuing Resolution. A congressional resolution passed in order to provide temporary funding for an agency, usually at the same level as the previous year, until its new appropriation is enacted.

Contraction. The phase of a business cycle when economic activity is declining. The period of time between a peak and a trough.

Cost-of-Living Adjustment (COLA). Adjustments to wages, benefits, or other payments that are based on a recently prevailing rate of inflation. Often automatic, they are meant to maintain the purchasing power of the affected wages, benefits, or payments.

Cost-Shifting. Occurs when hospitals charge patients with private health insurance higher fees for procedures because government reimbursements to hospitals for charges incurred by Medicare patients are below the hospital's cost of providing the procedure. Health insurance companies typically pass on the higher costs to customers in the form of higher health insurance premiums.

Crowd Out. A reduction in planned investment spending that occurs when increased federal government borrowing (to finance an increased budget deficit) causes interest rates to rise.

Cyclical Unemployment. Unemployment caused by the recession phase of the business cycle.

Deduction. Individual expenditures (e.g., on interest for a home mortgage, state and local tax payments, etc.) that under federal tax law can be used to reduce an individual's taxable income.

Deferral. A mechanism employed by presidents to delay the spending of congressionally appropriated funds.

Deflation. A negative rate of inflation. Occurs when aggregate prices decline over time.

Depression. A severe economic contraction during which economic activity declines to a very deep trough.

Deregulation. Reduction or elimination of government regulations.

Discount Rate. The interest rate charged by the Federal Reserve when it lends reserves to banks in order to assist banks in meeting mandated reserve requirements.

Discount Window Lending. The mechanism through which the Federal Reserve lends reserves to banks facing reserve shortfalls. May also be used by the Fed to regulate the money supply.

Discretionary Spending. Spending not mandated by existing laws.

Durable Good. A consumer good designed to provide benefits to its owner for three or more years. Examples include cars and refrigerators.

Earmark. Language in an appropriations bill that requires a specified amount of money to be spent in a specified way and place.

Entitlements. Mandatory government spending and loan programs that provide specific benefits to individuals based on predetermined qualifications (e.g., Social Security, veterans' pensions). Annual entitlement expenditures are determined jointly by the number of people who qualify and apply for the program plus the costs of the mandated benefits.

Excise Taxes. Amounts paid to the government at time of purchase by purchasers of goods such as tobacco, liquor, gasoline, and certain luxury items.

Exemptions. Predetermined amounts of an individual's income that are exempted from federal income taxes.

Expansion. The phase of a business cycle during which economic activity is increasing. This is the period of time between a trough and a peak.

Export Subsidy. A government subsidy to businesses exporting goods. Subsidies may be calculated as a percent of the value of the export or as a flat amount per unit.

Exports. Domestically produced goods and services sold to foreigners.

Externality. This exists when prices determined in the free market fail to reflect all the costs of production or all of the benefits that the product generates. In this case some of the costs or benefits affect third parties to the transaction.

Federal Funds Market. A market where banks with excess reserves lend them, overnight, to other banks with inadequate reserves.

Federal Funds Rate. The rate of interest that banks charge other banks on overnight loans of excess reserves.

Fee Caps. Government-specified limits on the prices it will pay for a wide variety of health care services provided to patients in the Medicare program.

Fiscal Policy. Annual decisions about federal spending and revenues and the consequent deficit or surplus.

Fiscal Year. For budgetary purposes the government year runs from October 1 to September 30 of the following calendar year. Each fiscal year takes the number of the calendar year in which it ends.

Free Market Economy. An economy structured so that aggregate decisions of individual buyers and sellers determine both the amounts and kinds of goods and services that are produced, the methods of production utilized, and the prices that will be charged for each good and service.

Frictional Unemployment. Unemployment that results when people with job skills are in the process of voluntarily switching jobs. Because it usually takes time to obtain information on job opportunities and to relocate, there is sometimes a temporary period of unemployment when people switch jobs.

General Agreement on Tariffs and Trade (GATT). An international trade treaty that aims to promote free trade through limits on the use of export subsidies, import quotas, and tariffs.

Government Spending. Total purchases of goods and services by federal, state, and local governments.

Gramm-Rudman-Hollings Act (GRH). A law enacted in 1985 requiring annual reductions in federal budget deficits until a balanced budget was reached in 1991. The law mandated an automatic reduction in government spending when the president and Congress were unable to agree on how to meet the targeted reductions in the deficit.

Gross Domestic Product (GDP). The sum of the current purchase prices of all final goods and services produced in the domestic economy in a given time period.

Horizontal Regulation. Occurs when a federal agency is assigned to regulate a specific kind of economic behavior across different industries (e.g., regulation of occupational health and safety).

Hyperinflation. Very large and rapid increases in prices that make people unwilling to hold cash because its purchasing power declines so quickly.

Import Quota. A government-mandated limit on the quantity of a specific good that can be imported in a given time period.

Imports. Foreign-produced goods and services sold domestically.

Impoundments. Deferrals or rescissions.

Indexing. A mechanism for increasing government benefit payments and wages as inflation rises so that the purchasing power of the payment does not decline.

Industrial Policy. A formal government tax, spending, or regulatory policy aimed at encouraging the growth of specific industries.

Inflation Rate. The percentage rate of change in the level of prices as measured by a given price index.

Investment. Output purchased by the business sector, including machinery, factory and office buildings. Also includes expenditures for the purchase of new homes.

Laffer Curve. A graphical representation of the relationship between tax rates and government tax revenues. It suggests that at very high tax rates, government revenues can actually be increased by reducing tax rates.

Local-Content Requirement. A government regulation requiring that some specified fraction of a retail good be produced domestically.

M1. A measure of the money supply equal to the sum of cash in circulation, travelers' checks, and all funds in checking accounts.

M2. A broader measure of money equal to the sum of M1 plus funds in money market mutual funds, money market deposit accounts, small certificates of deposit, and other investments.

Macroeconomists. Individuals who study the performance of the economy as a whole as measured by unemployment, output of goods and services, inflation, and other factors.

Marginal Rates. Also known as marginal tax rates. The fraction of additional taxable income that must be paid in taxes.

Market. A structured environment in which buyers and sellers engage in the voluntary exchange of goods and services, usually for money.

Marketable Security. A formal, interest-bearing IOU, initially issued by governments or corporations, that can be resold to other buyers in a secondary market. Includes U.S. Treasury bills, notes, and bonds.

Microeconomic Policy. Government decisions that directly affect a particular segment of the economy, including such things as regulation, subsidies, bailouts, and focused loan programs.

Monetarism. A school of economic thought that views price instability as the primary macroeconomic problem and relatively stable money growth as the optimal policy to maintain price stability.

Monetary Policy. Government decisions about the supply of money available to the economy and the rates charged to borrowers to use it.

Multiplier Effect. The process by which a small change in consumption, investment, net exports, government spending, or taxes may cause a much larger change in national output.

National Debt. The total amount of money that the federal government has borrowed over the years but has not yet repaid.

Natural Rate Hypothesis. An economic theory stating that in the long run the unemployment rate will be equal to the natural rate of unemployment. Consequently, there is no long-run trade-off between inflation and unemployment.

Natural Rate of Unemployment. This is the sum of frictional and structural unemployment. It is the amount of unemployment that would occur when there is no cyclical unemployment.

Net Exports. Goods and services produced in the United States and sold in foreign countries minus goods and services produced in foreign countries that are purchased by people living in the United States.

Net Interest. See Debt Service.

Nominal GDP. See Gross Domestic Product.

Nondurable Good. A consumer good designed to provide benefits to its owner for less than three years. Examples include shampoo and food.

Nonmarketable Security. A formal, interest-bearing IOU, initially issued by governments or corporations, that cannot be resold to other buyers in a secondary market. Includes U.S. savings bonds.

North American Free Trade Agreement (NAFTA). An international trade treaty among Canada, Mexico, and the United States that promotes free trade by substantially reducing tariffs on goods imported from any of the signatories.

Open-Market Operations. A purchase or sale of Treasury bills, notes, or bonds in the secondary market by the Federal Reserve for the purpose of controlling the money supply.

Outlays. Appropriations that have been designated for spending in a particular fiscal year.

Pay-as-you-go. A budgetary principle requiring that bills increasing the deficit through either increases in discretionary spending or decreases in revenues be accompanied by off-setting adjustments elsewhere so that the net impact on the deficit is zero.

Payroll Taxes. Money withheld from individual paychecks for specific programs such as Social Security or Medicare. Sometimes called social insurance receipts.

Peak. A turning point in the business cycle when the expansion phase ends and the recession phase begins.

Phillips Curve. A representation of the relationship between inflation and unemployment.

Political Action Committee (PAC). The political arm of a special-interest group. A PAC becomes influential by making campaign contributions to candidates sympathetic to the group's position.

Populists. Largely agrarian members of a nineteenth-century political movement that favored increased government regulation of the economy, particularly for the purpose of stabilizing prices.

Pork-Barrel Spending. Federal expenditures on specific projects in the states or districts of individual members of Congress that are carried out for their direct benefits and for the political support they are likely to engender.

Price Index. An average of the prices of a predetermined variety of products computed at specific points in time. Usually calculated on a standardized scale with a value of 100 at the predetermined reference point.

Primary Market. A market in which investors can buy newly issued marketable or nonmarketable securities.

Prime Rate. The interest rate banks charge on loans to their best corporate customers.

Progressive Movement. A late-1800s–early-1900s political movement with a largely urban membership that favored a broader distribution of economic and political power.

Public Goods. These are goods, such as national defense and roads, that are indivisible among individuals. It is impossible to limit consumption of these goods to those people who have paid their share of the costs.

Real Budget Deficit. The amount by which government expenditures exceed government revenues, based on the value of a dollar in an agreed-upon year.

Real GDP. The sum of all final goods and services produced in the domestic economy in a given time period but with the purchase prices of each good or service computed on the basis of the value of the dollar in an agreed-upon year.

Receipts. The money government collects from all sources to fund its operations. Includes revenues and funds obtained by borrowing.

Recession. The phase of a business cycle when economic activity is declining. The period of time between a peak and a trough.

Recognition Lag. The amount of time that elapses before policymakers recognize that the economy has arrived at a turning point in the business cycle.

Reconciliation. A concurrent resolution, passed by the House and Senate, that reconciles specific amounts to be spent in the coming fiscal year with the overall budget ceiling.

Red-Tape Barrier. An informal mechanism employed by governments to restrict imports by utilizing health, safety, or customs procedures to create substantial obstacles to trade.

Required Reserves. The minimum amount of funds that banks and other depository institutions (e.g., credit unions) are required to keep in an account with the Federal Reserve or as cash in the bank's vault.

Required Reserve Ratio. A fraction mandated by the Federal Reserve. This fraction multiplied by a bank's deposits determines the amount of required reserves a bank must hold.

Rescissions. A tool employed by presidents to block the spending of congressionally appropriated funds.

Revenues. Government receipts derived from taxes, tariffs, and fees.

Secondary Market. A market in which investors can buy or sell previously issued marketable securities.

Sequester. A mandatory, across-the-board spending cut of previously appropriated funds.

Services. Consumer products that are not manufactured. Examples include haircuts and doctors' visits.

Spending Caps. Congressionally imposed limits on discretionary federal spending.

Stagflation. Rising prices accompanied by rising unemployment and slow rates of economic growth.

Stock Market. A secondary market in which investors buy and sell shares of ownership (i.e., stocks) of thousands of different corporations.

Structural Deficit. This is a hypothetical concept that measures the expected size of the annual budget deficit if the unemployment rate during the year remained at the natural rate of employment (i.e., 6 percent).

Structural Unemployment. Unemployment that is usually involuntary and that results from a mismatch of skilled labor and job vacancies. The mismatches are typically geographic or skills related.

Supply-Side Economics. A school of economic thought that views slow productivity growth as the primary macroeconomic problem and reduced government regulation as well as tax cuts that encourage work and investment as the optimal economic policy response.

Tariff. A tax levied on imported goods. May be calculated as a percent of the value of the product or a flat tax per unit.

Tax Brackets. Predetermined ranges of taxable income. Higher marginal tax rates are assessed for higher tax brackets.

Tax Expenditures. An exemption or deduction granted by tax law in order to encourage certain kinds of behavior that alternatively could be encouraged through the payment of government subsidies.

Tax Refund. A payment made by the government to individuals who have paid taxes in excess of what they owed.

Trade Balance. The monetary value of the difference between exports and imports.

Trade Deficit. The amount by which imports exceed exports.

Trade Surplus. The amount by which exports exceed imports.

Treasury Bills. Marketable securities sold by the U.S. Treasury Department as a means to borrow money to finance budget deficits and refinance outstanding debt of the U.S. government. Bills have maturities of three months to one year.

Treasury Bonds. Marketable securities sold by the U.S. Treasury Department as a means to borrow money to finance budget deficits and refinance outstanding debt of the U.S. government. Bonds have maturities greater than ten years.

Treasury Notes. Marketable securities sold by the U.S. Treasury Department as a means to borrow money to finance budget deficits and refinance outstanding debt of the U.S. government. Notes have maturities of two to ten years.

Trough. A turning point in the business cycle when the recession phase ends and the expansion phase begins.

Trusts. Groups of late-nineteenth-century corporations, in the same industry, that operated as an individual business to reduce the costs of competition for the purpose of increasing their profits.

Unemployment Rate. The percentage of people in the labor force who are both available for work and actively seeking work but are unable to find a job.

Vertical Regulation. Occurs when a federal agency is assigned to regulate different kinds of economic behavior within a single industry.

Voluntary Export Restraint (VER). A voluntary limit, accepted by businesses in a foreign country, on the quantity of a specific good that they will export in a given time period.

Notes

Chapter 1

1. Computed from the average change in real GDP growth rates from 1946 to 1993.

2. For BLS purposes civilians include all people over the age of sixteen who are not confined to an institution (prison, mental hospital, etc.). People in the military are not counted as part of the labor force because they are always fully employed.

3. When GDP is measured, government spending does not include transfer programs. A transfer program is one where the government collects money from one segment of the population for the express purpose of transferring it to a different segment of the population. The government does not purchase anything, it merely redistributes income in society. For example, Social Security involves a transfer of income from working people to retired people.

4. To compute the rate of inflation in consumer prices over a given time period, say, the years 1970–1980, we would use this equation:

$$\text{Inflation Rate} = \frac{\text{CPI}_{1980} - \text{CPI}_{1970}}{\text{CPI}_{1970}} \times 100 = \frac{82.4 - 38.8}{38.8} \times 100 = 112.37\%$$

During this period of time the prices of typical products more than doubled.

5. Other factors also affect business investment (e.g., U.S. government tax policy, expectations regarding inflation, etc.) and can mitigate interest-rate effects on unemployment and economic growth.

6. These paragraphs focus on traditional Keynesian theory because it was the basis of much macroeconomic policy conducted in the United States in the post–World War II period. Modifications to the theory were made to correct problems with the original theories that were discovered in the 1970s. This new approach is called neo-Keynesian economics and incorporates more of a focus on the long-run impacts of macroeconomic policy.

7. Politicians are not unanimous in their support of this position, although most economists are. In February 1994 Senator Paul Sarbanes responded to the Federal Reserve's modest 0.25 percent increase in a short-term interest rate by comparing the Fed to "a bomber coming along and striking a farmhouse . . . because you think that the villain inflation is inside . . . when in fact what's inside . . . is a happy family appreciating the restoration of economic growth" (from the *Wall Street Journal*, "Common Interest: President and Fed Seem in Step on Latest Rate Rise," by David Wessel, February, 17, 1994, pp. A1, A6.)

Chapter 2

1. Trusts were declared illegal by the Sherman Antitrust Act of 1890.

2. In the early years after their passage, both the Interstate Commerce Act and the Sherman Act were rendered largely ineffective by court decisions that most often sided with business interests against the regulators.

3. Unless otherwise indicated, all data in this chapter are from U.S. Department of Commerce, Bureau of the Census, *Historical Statistics of the United States: Colonial Times to 1970* (Washington, D.C.: Government Printing Office, 1975) or U.S. Department of Commerce, Bureau of the Census, *Statistical Abstract of the United States, 1993* (Washington, D.C.: Government Printing Office, 1993).

4. Speech at Oglethorpe University, Atlanta, Georgia, May 22, 1932.

Chapter 3

1. A capital gain occurs when an individual sells a previously purchased financial asset (e.g., a house, stocks, bonds, etc.) at a profit. The profit (i.e., capital gain) is taxed at rates determined by Congress.

2. Many people still share the misbelief that our money supply is backed by gold or some other precious metal. It isn't. Neither are there huge government warehouses of currency that fully back our money supply. When the public chooses to hold more currency and keep less in deposits (e.g., around Christmastime) the Fed makes more currency available. However, most people prefer to hold most of their money in the form of deposits rather than as currency. These factors make it easy for the Fed to create new money simply by creating new deposits.

3. See Froyen and Greer, *Principles of Macroeconomics,* pp. 307–313, for a more detailed explanation of this process.

Chapter 4

1. A useful metaphor for this problem follows. Suppose you're driving a car with finicky brakes. Sometimes when you hit the brakes the car stops immediately, sometimes it stops thirty seconds later, and other times it stops two minutes later. Now, imagine you are approaching a very busy intersection. You are a block away and the light turns red. What should you do? If you apply your brake you might stop right where you are, you might stop at the intersection, or the car might not stop until after you burst through the red light.

2. For example, changes in the consumer price index (CPI) tend to overstate the true rate of inflation because the CPI rises when (1) goods of unchanging quality (e.g., corn flakes) cost more and (2) the quality of products rises and so does their purchase price (e.g., new cars with airbags installed). In the latter case, price increases are not measuring inflation but the higher costs of a better product.

3. This effect could be fully offset if individual savings increased enough to offset the increased government demand for credit. However, in the United States since the 1960s the opposite has occurred as private savings actually declined from 8 percent of GDP to 5 percent of GDP. This, combined with rising deficits, has caused the supply of savings available for private investment to decline from about 8 percent of GDP to only 2 percent of GDP (Bipartisan Commission on Entitlement and Tax Reform, 1994).

4. During a recession the real GDP growth rate falls. Simultaneously, automatic fiscal stabilizers cause the deficit to increase, which usually results in a surge in the growth rate of real debt.

Chapter 5

1. This occurs because most current retirees paid Social Security taxes when these tax rates were lower but collect their checks years later after several rounds of very generous benefit increases.

2. From Medicare's specification of diagnostic related groups (DRG). This is DRG # 121: A circulatory disorder with anterior myocardial infarction.

3. In 1993 the median family income was $31,700. Defining the middle-class as 50 percent of all families equally distributed around the median implies that middle-class families earn between $14,040 and $55,880 (Peterson, 1993: p. 30).

References

Associated Press. "Dole: Bush Should Act Now on Plan to Revive the Economy." *Washington Post*, November 30, 1991, p. A10.

Bipartisan Commission on Entitlement and Tax Reform. *First Report of the Bipartisan Commission on Entitlement and Tax Reform.* Washington, D.C.: Government Printing Office, 1994.

Birnbaum, Jeffrey H., and Alan S. Murray. *Showdown at Gucci Gulch: Lawmakers, Lobbyists and the Unlikely Triumph of Tax Reform.* New York: Random House, 1987.

Calmes, Jackie. " 'F-Word' Threatens Clinton Capitol Hill Agenda, Though Wind Has Gone Out of Most Filibusters." *Wall Street Journal*, August 16, 1994, p. A14.

Campagna, Anthony S. *U.S. National Economic Policy, 1917–1985.* New York: Praeger, 1985.

Chang, Roberto, "Income Inequality and Economic Growth: Evidence and Recent Theories." In Federal Reserve Bank of Atlanta, *Economic Review*, July/August 1994.

Clinton, Bill, and Al Gore. *Putting People First: How We Can All Change America.* New York: Times Books, 1992.

Congressional Budget Office. *Reducing Entitlement Spending.* Washington, D.C.: Government Printing Office, 1994.

Congressional Quarterly Weekly Report. *Special Report: Where the Money Goes,* December 11, 1993.

Denison, Edward F. *Trends in American Economic Growth.* Washington, D.C.: Brookings Institution, 1985.

Devroy, Anne, and E. J. Dionne Jr. "Bush Team Regroups After Week of Turmoil," *Washington Post*, November 23, 1991, pp. A1, A11.

Economic Report of the President. Washington, D.C.: Government Printing Office, various years.

Finkelstein, Joseph. *The American Economy: From the Great Crash to the Third Industrial Revolution.* Arlington Heights, Ill.: Harlan Davidson, 1992.

Friedman, Milton, and Anna J. Schwartz. *A Monetary History of the United States, 1867–1960.* Chicago: University of Chicago Press, 1963.

Froyen Richard T., and Douglas F. Greer. *Principles of Macroeconomics.* New York: Macmillan, 1989.

Galambos, Louis, and Joseph Pratt. *The Rise of the Corporate Commonwealth: U.S. Business and Public Policy in the Twentieth Century.* New York: Basic Books, 1988.

George, Peter. *The Emergence of Industrial America.* Albany: State University of New York Press, 1982.

Germond, Jack W., and Jules Witcover. *Mad as Hell: Revolt at the Ballot Box, 1992.* New York: Warner Books, 1993.

Greenspan, Alan. "Statement Before a Joint Hearing of the Senate and House Committees on the Budget." *Federal Reserve Bulletin*, March 1995.

Greider, William. "The Education of David Stockman." *Atlantic,* December 1981.

Harwood, John. "Journal/NBC Poll Finds Further Drop in Bush's Rating." *Wall Street Journal,* December 12, 1991, p. A16.

Hofstadter, Richard. *The Age of Reform: From Bryan to F.D.R.* New York: Alfred A. Knopf, 1955.

Hoover, Herbert. *The Challenge to Liberty.* New York: Charles Scribner's Sons, 1934.

Howe, Neil, and Phillip Longman. "The Next New Deal." *Atlantic,* April, 1992.

International Monetary Fund. *International Financial Statistics,* April 1995.

Kemp, Tom. *The Climax of Capitalism: The U.S. Economy in the Twentieth Century.* New York: Longman, 1990.

Krugman, Paul. *Peddling Prosperity.* New York: Norton, 1994.

Krugman, Paul R., and Maurice Obstfeld. *International Economics: Theory and Policy.* New York: HarperCollins College Publishers, 1994.

Leuchtenberg, William E. *The Perils of Prosperity.* Chicago: University of Chicago Press, 1958.

Lindert, Peter H. *International Economics.* Homewood, Ill.: Richard D. Irwin, 1991.

Lyons, Eugene. *Herbert Hoover: A Biography.* Garden City, N.Y.: Doubleday, 1964.

McQueen, Michael. "Voters Demand Political Leaders Do Something, Almost Anything, to Spur Economic Recovery." *Wall Street Journal,* December 13, 1991, p. A16.

Meltzer, Allan H. "Limits of Short-run Stabilization Policy." *Economic Inquiry* 25, no. 1, 1987, pp. 1–14.

Meyers, Roy T. *Strategic Budgeting.* Ann Arbor: University of Michigan Press, 1994.

Motley, Brian. "New Measures of the Work Force." *Federal Reserve Bank of San Francisco Weekly Letter* no. 94-11, March 18, 1994.

Pae, Peter. "President Urges Banks to Lower Rates on Credit Cards to Stimulate Spending." *Wall Street Journal,* November 13, 1991, pp. A3–4.

Peterson, Peter G. *Facing Up.* New York: Simon and Schuster, 1993.

Pound, Edward T., and Douglas Pasternak. "The Pork Barrel Barons." *US News and World Report,* February 21, 1994, p. 32.

Schlesinger, Arthur M., Jr. *A Thousand Days.* Boston: Houghton Mifflin, 1965.

Schultze, Charles L. *Memos to the President: A Guide Through Macroeconomics for the Busy Policymaker.* Washington, D.C.: Brookings Institution, 1992.

Schuman, Howard E. *Politics and the Budget: The Struggle Between the President and the Congress.* Englewood Cliffs, N.J.: Prentice-Hall, 1992.

Seib, Gerald F. "Cutting Spending Isn't So Easy: Another Lesson." *Wall Street Journal,* July 6, 1994, p. A20.

Smith, Hedrick. *The Power Game: How Washington Works.* New York: Random House, 1988.

Stein, Herbert. *Presidential Economics.* Washington, D.C.: American Enterprise Institute Press, 1994.

Tarr, David G. *A General Equilibrium Analysis of the Welfare and Employment Effects of U.S. Quotas in Textiles, Autos, and Steel.* Washington, D.C.: Federal Trade Commission, 1989.

Tarr, David G., and Morris E. Morkre. *Costs to the United States of Tariffs and Quotas on Imports.* Washington, D.C.: Federal Trade Commission, 1984.

Thomas, Paulette. "Bipartisan Panel Outlines Evils of Entitlements, but Hint of Benefit Cuts Spurs Stiff Opposition." *Wall Street Journal,* August 8, 1994, p. A14.

Turner, Frederick Jackson. *The Frontier in American History.* New York: Henry Holt, 1921.

U.S. Department of Commerce, Bureau of the Census. *Statistical Abstract of the United States, 1993, 1994.* Washington, D.C.: Government Printing Office, 1993, 1994.

Weiner, Tim. "Sending Money to Home Districts: Earmarking and the Pork Barrel." *New York Times,* July 13, 1994, p. A1.

Wessel, David. "Common Interest: President and Fed Seem in Step on Latest Rate Rise." *Wall Street Journal,* February, 17, 1994, pp. A1, A6.

Woodward, Bob. *The Agenda.* New York: Simon and Schuster, 1994.

Wyrick, Thomas L. *The Economist's Handbook: A Research and Writing Guide.* St. Paul: West, 1994.

About the Book and Authors

FOR YEARS NOW, Americans have called for a balanced budget, debt reduction, and fiscal sanity. Yet the federal government continues to spend beyond its income, driving the level of federal debt up and public confidence down. Why is that? Why have the monsters of public finance—pork-barrel spending, entitlements, and the deficit—remained unchecked for so long? What effects have they had on our economy and our politics? What, if anything, can be done to tame them?

This concise, well-written primer of American political economy offers answers to these questions and more, all the while covering a vast and complicated intellectual terrain in an accessible and engaging way. Political scientist Cal Mackenzie and economist Saranna Thornton combine forces here to clear up some of the mysteries of contemporary economic theory and practice. They take us on a sweeping tour of the economic turning points in our national history and then go on to discuss what it will take to make sound economic policy and, ultimately, good government for the twenty-first century.

Everyone—but especially students of American government, public policy, economics, and business—should have a copy of this on the shelf to help them make sense of the economic news and its political ramifications.

G. Calvin Mackenzie holds the endowed chair of Distinguished Presidential Professor of American Government at Colby College. **Saranna Thornton** is assistant professor of economics, also at Colby College.

Index